The Open University

U213

International Development:
Challenges for a World in Transition

Introduction to

DISPLACEMENT

Prepared for the Course Team by Jenny Robinson
and Vandana Desai

Cover photo Rwandan refugees returning home, Tanzania/Rwanda border, 1996.

The Open University
Walton Hall
Milton Keynes
MK7 6AA
United Kingdom

First published 2001. Reprinted 2003

Edited, designed and typeset by The Open University

Printed in the United Kingdom by The Alden Group, Oxford

ISBN 0 7492 3811 9

This publication forms part of an Open University course U213 *International Development: Challenges for a World in Transition*

Details of this and other Open University courses can be obtained from the Call Centre, PO Box 724, The Open University, Milton Keynes, MK7 6ZS, United Kingdom, tel. +44 (0)1908 653231, email ces-gen@open.ac.uk. Alternatively, you may visit the Open University website at http://www.open.ac.uk where you can learn more about the wide range of courses and packs offered at all levels by the Open University

If you have not already enrolled on the course and would like to purchase this or other Open University material, contact Open University Worldwide Ltd, The Berrill Building, Walton Hall, Milton Keynes MK7 6AA, United Kingdom: tel. +44 (0)1908 858785; fax +44 (0)1908 858787; email ouwenq@open.ac.uk; website http://www.ouw.co.uk

1.2

Contents

Theme Introductions

Displacement is one of the five Themes you will cover whilst studying this course. The other four Themes are: *Transitions, Poverty and Inequality, Technology and Knowledge*, and *Sustainability*.

Five weeks of study are set aside during Part 1 of U213 for these Theme Introductions, each comprising one week. You are expected to study them after you have completed your study of *Poverty and Development into the 21st Century* (Allen and Thomas, 2000; hereafter called the Course Book) and its associated audiocassettes, as directed by *Study Guide 1*. At the end of this five-week period a further week is set aside for you to complete tutor-marked assignment TMA 03 and to make your Theme choices for Part 2 of the course.

Remember that in Part 2 you will study *three* of the five Themes in the following order:

> *Transitions* (compulsory Theme)
>
> *Poverty and Inequality* or *Technology and Knowledge*
>
> *Displacement* or *Sustainability*.

The final section of *Study Guide 1* provides information that should help you make your choices. You should return to this once you have completed your study of the Theme Introductions.

Even if you are already certain which Themes you intend to study in Part 2 you should study all five Introductions in Part 1, including this one. This is because each Introduction practises skills that are relevant to other Themes and, also, we expect you to obtain a rounded view before you specialize. You may be assessed in your final examination on the learning outcomes associated with any of the Introductions. You will also be encouraged to illustrate TMA 03 with examples from a range of the Themes.

The Theme Introductions are self-contained, although, as noted above, they all assume that you have completed your study of the Course Book and its associated audiocassettes. We recommend, however, that you study them during this five-week period in the following order:

First week   *Transitions*

Second week   *Poverty and Inequality*

Third week   *Technology and Knowledge*

Fourth week   *Displacement*

Fifth week   *Sustainability*

The sixth week has been set aside for completing TMA 03 and making your choices for Part 2 of the course.

Studying *Introduction to Displacement*

Some general aims of this Introduction are presented below. We also provide a checklist of learning outcomes. These are what we expect you to be able to do once you have completed the Introduction and are what you are potentially assessed upon in your TMAs and/or final examination.

The main text, which follows the outline of the aims, skills and learning outcomes, contains activities for you to undertake. These are included to engage you *actively* with the text and to foster deeper-level study than you will be able to achieve simply by reading. Typically these activities check that you understand what is being written and can critically engage with the material, and draw you into the process of developing the text argument. Do therefore attempt to do the activities before reading the commentaries that follow them. The main text also directs you from time to time to the Course Book, so make sure that you always have this to hand.

The *Introduction to Displacement* should take approximately one week of your study time for this course.

Aims and skills

The aim of this Introduction is to help you to understand how to:
- explore the significance of flows and networks within contemporary society;
- consider the role of place and displacement in development thinking and practice;
- assess the implications of displacement for development practice.

It also helps you to develop the following skills:
- *Knowledge* and awareness of the ways in which development thinking has been territorialized around the local, national and global, and of the relationships between places and displacement, or flows and territories.
- *Conceptual skills* to help you analyse key issues and arguments concerning place and displacement, and specific concepts useful in their interpretation, such as territory, scale, flows and borders.
- *Key skills* (data, maps, images).
- *Numerical skills* in the interpretation of tables.
- *Visual skills* in the interpretation of video, maps and photographs.

These skills are only developed to a basic level in this Introduction. They, and other skills, will be developed further in Part 2 of the *Displacement* Theme.

Learning outcomes

After studying *Introduction to Displacement* you should be able to do the following:

- Explain why displacement of various kinds matters to the understanding of development.
- Examine flows of people, ideas and things in the context of places and territories.
- Discuss why places are important in livelihoods and opportunities for development.
- Evaluate the significance of displacement for development thinking and practice.
- Assess the implications of human mobility.
- Reflect critically on development-induced displacements and their amelioration.

1 What is this Theme about?

1.1 Things and people on the move

At the turn of the twenty-first century, many of the striking issues of poverty and development which reach an international audience involve displacement in one way or another. Wars, famines and big dam developments are perhaps the most prominent examples, all of which leave many people dislocated, having had to leave their homes, neighbourhoods and perhaps even their countries in the search of safety, or what Tim Allen (1996) called 'cool ground'. Some of the more politically controversial work of international relief and development agencies has been concerned with addressing the immediate humanitarian needs of displaced communities and then, in the longer term, initiating development projects aimed at post-conflict reconstruction, for example, or famine prevention. Often, though, it is the images of refugees and aid workers in emergency camps which capture the imagination (and the donations) of the global public (Figure 1.1).

Figure 1.1 Aid workers helping Rwandan refugees returning home over the Tanzania/Rwanda border, 1996.

While *refugees* across the world in recent years have been estimated at varying between 10 million and 17 million during the 1990s, and *internally displaced* people at between 10 million to 18 million during the 1980s and 1990s (Course Book, Chapter 8), the number of people estimated to have been *resettled* to make way for development initiatives has been put at around 100 million over the ten-year period from 1988. At the same time as relief and development agencies are battling to respond to the complexities of political and environmental emergencies that cause displacement, and their longer-term consequences for poverty, many more people are arguably being displaced in the name of development.

One of the more prominent examples of development displacement is big dam construction. Perhaps you are familiar with some of the high profile public campaigns against dam developments, such as the Narmada Dam in India, against which prominent public figures, such as Arundhati Roy[*], have been lobbying. But there are others. Michael Cernea and Christopher McDowell (2000) write that involuntary resettlers have been uprooted by development-inducing programmes such as 'infrastructure construction for industrial estates, dams and reservoirs, highways, ports and airports, urban transportation networks. Unlike refugees, people resettled as a result of development projects typically remain inside national borders' (p.1). Nonetheless, they continue, 'contrary to expectations, development programmes that are supposed to widely improve living standards have also brought, under the wings of progress, the forced displacement of millions and millions of poor and vulnerable people in many of the world's developing countries, inducing impoverishment and hardship' (p.2). It is not simply being displaced from one's homeland which is a source of hardship; long-standing and hard-won livelihoods and social networks forged in particular places are disrupted by resettlement. And it is seldom those who are displaced who are expected to be the beneficiaries of the development in question.

[*]Arundhati Roy is the award-winning Indian author of *The God of Small Things.*

Even as the astonishing figures of people involuntarily displaced for various reasons seem to offer cause for alarm, there are many writers and popular commentators who see the present era of global capitalism as intrinsically characterized by mobility and displacement. People, goods, cultural products, communications, ideas – these are all seen to be on the move, and in ways which are usually thought about as broadly positive. Many commentators celebrate the idea that in the sphere of culture and identity we are seeing the emergence of a '*world in creolization*'[*] (Hannerz, 1996) and cultural hybridity is thought of as a positive outcome of the movement of people around the world. Moreover, as Gupta and Ferguson (1999, p.38) note, 'it is not only the displaced who experience displacement'. They refer to the experience of post-colonial Britain, where notions of 'Britishness' and 'Englishness' have been transformed by the immigration of people from many different parts of the former empire. English people who have never moved anywhere are experiencing a sense of displacement as their identities and their cultural worlds are effectively hybridized.

[*]Creolization: the process whereby all cultures are comprised of influences from many different parts of the world. 'Creole' has previously been used to refer to specific cultures or languages which developed out of the mixing of colonizers and colonized people.

In the economic realm, technological advancements mean that money and information can be sent around the world in seconds and firms can spread their activities around the globe without losing the capacity to co-ordinate and manage their operations effectively. As John Harriss discussed in Chapter 15 of the Course Book, this technological revolution has underpinned major changes in the global economy (p.336). These same changes in communications technology are also behind the challenges confronting many local cultures in the face of global forces (p.502, Chapter 23 in the Course Book). Many of the changes which we can identify in the global political economy can be said to contribute to different forms of what we want to call '*displacement*'.

We are using the term 'displacement' very broadly here, to refer not only to human displacement, but also to the movement of goods, activities and ideas around the world.

Of course the two types of movement are related. Human migrations (whether forced removals or voluntary migrations) are closely related to the broader processes which enable the distribution and circulation of economic activities and cultural forms. Many of the processes which make up 'globalization' are those which shape what the Course Book (Chapter 2) calls spontaneous or '*immanent development*' – so changing patterns of the movement of ideas, goods and people are intrinsically bound up with processes of 'development'.

This is clearly evident in one of the most significant examples of human displacement in history, which is usually thought of as involving 'voluntary' migration – the movement of people to urban areas. Castles and Miller suggest that:

> The first effect of foreign investment and development is rural–urban migration, and the growth of cities. Leaving traditional forms of production and social relationships to move into burgeoning cities is the first stage of fundamental social, psychological and cultural changes, which create the pre-dispositions for further migrations. To move from peasant agriculture into a city like Manila, Sao Paulo or Lagos may be a bigger step for many than the subsequent move to a 'global city' like Tokyo, New York or Sydney.
>
> (Castles and Miller, 1993, p.165)

This form of human displacement is expected to continue at a rapid rate for the foreseeable future (Figure 1.2).

Much of the urbanization which is now taking place in the world is happening in poorer countries, posing a serious challenge to *intentional development* efforts (see Chapter 2 of the Course Book). More than two-thirds of the world's urban population are now in Africa, Asia, Latin America and the Caribbean. Between 1950 and 1995, the urban population of these regions grew more than fivefold – from 346 million to 1.8 billion. Although Asia and Africa still have more rural than urban dwellers, they both have very large urban populations. Asia alone has close to half the world's urban population – with more than half of its urban population within just two countries, China and India.* Africa

*In Chapter 20 of the Course Book, Jo Beall considers how increased global connections have contributed to urban migration (p.433), and the cosmopolitan diversity of populations found in most large cities around the world is testimony to this.

Figure 1.2 Traffic congestion in rapidly urbanizing Kathmandu, 1997.

now has a larger urban population than Northern America; so too does Latin America and the Caribbean. Moreover, South and Central America have close to three-quarters of their population living in urban centres. Large-scale human movements to cities are changing the landscape of the globe, and the nature of challenges facing development.

The second section of this Introduction (a case study of development displacement in Mumbai) will explore some aspects of urbanization in India.

1.2 Or trapped in place?

Even as you read this, you may have called to mind the often bitter political conflicts which surround debates over the rights of migrants or refugees to enter wealthier countries. 'Mobility' may be celebrated in the West as the basis of the contemporary global economy, but the movement of people across national borders, especially those of wealthier Western countries, is increasingly strictly controlled. You might recall from both John Harriss's chapter in the Course Book and Chapter 16 by Anthony McGrew that globalization (a definition is in Box 16.1 on p.347) may mean faster communications, more opportunity for mobility, and more and deeper links between places. But you might also recall that the consequences of all this movement are not always positive in terms of welfare or economic growth – some places lose out from globalization and inequalities across the globe are increasing. More than that, some people in some places do not have the opportunity to move – they may have little choice but to stay where they are. Refugees in many conflict situations are actively encouraged (coerced?) to remain in the region of the conflict, and to return home, rather than seek exile status in other, wealthier countries or even to settle permanently in safer neighbouring states. 'Fortress Europe', defended against unwanted migration, is a stark reminder that some kinds of movements are not always possible even as many experiences of mobility or displacement are far from desirable.

While the global political economy might seem to have become characterized by flows and displacements, there are also powerful forces at work which are re-emphasizing the importance of boundaries in economic and social life.

Older patterns and boundaries may be less important than they once were (e.g. nation-states) but new configurations are emerging which are setting new borders and limits to movement. Supra-national entities like the European Union (EU), for example, now set substantial limits to mobility across its frontiers, even as movement and trade within the EU are facilitated. So far, then, we have noted that:

- Mobility and displacement are not only significant in the current political and economic landscape; they are also deeply contested and complex in their impacts.
- Mobility may be a key feature of the contemporary capitalist economy, but it can also be harmful when it brings with it the erosion of local values or the loss of livelihoods.
- Movement and displacements may be a product of current changes in the global economy, but there are also new processes which settle people and limit their movement, not always in positive ways.

In sum, the late twentieth century and the early part of the twenty-first century have seen *a surge of interest in the phenomenon of global mobility*. The consequences of what has been called 'globalization' for all areas of life – economy, politics, culture – have drawn an enormous amount of popular and academic interest. Whether or not this actually involves a substantial transition from a more settled world of borders and nations to one where people and things are hypermobile and borders irrelevant (and some commentators vigorously contest these claims), there is no doubt that many areas of social life are being restructured in response to these processes. Governments insist that they have no choice but to make policy in ways that are compatible with global forces; firms seek opportunities for investment and trade across the globe, supported by on-going innovations in telecommunications (Figure 1.3); and people participate regularly in forms of media and culture drawn from all over the world. There is of course much debate as to whether there is no alternative than to bow to global economic forces, or whether global culture undermines local distinctiveness (many people argue just the opposite, that it promotes and stimulates new kinds of local identities, as Tim Allen notes in Chapter 21 of the Course Book). But at the very least there has been a shift in how global economy and culture are thought

Figure 1.3 Small rural holding with TV aerial, Cambodia, 2001.

about; the world is now seen to be more mobile and interconnected, which has also changed many people's actions and expectations.

1.3 Displacement and development

In this context, development and how we think about it have also had to change. Dramatic forced displacements are causing development and relief workers to question the significance of national borders and sovereignty. At the same time the growing globalization of the economy and the transnationalization of social life are posing substantial challenges to existing development thinking and practice.

Consider the case of humanitarian organizations, which are increasingly coming up against attempts to limit their actions across national borders, and who are consequently questioning restrictions on taking aid into nationally controlled territories. You might recall from *Study Guide 1*, Activity 20, a discussion of the audiocassette programme 'Whose Right to Intervene' in which Tim Allen interviewed the founder of Médecins

Sans Frontières, Bernard Kouchner, about recent UN legislation enabling humanitarian interventions across national borders. The concerns and practices of humanitarian and aid workers are part of the challenges to the borders and divisions which characterize the existing form of global politics based on a system of nation-states. Similarly, many national communities are spread across the world, forming diasporic[*] networks and retaining close ties and national identifications, but who are not contained within the physical borders of the nation-state.

These examples pose a number of questions for development thought and practice:

■ Should practices of development be imagined as a type of diasporic activity as well, drawing on globally dispersed networks and relationships to improve well-being, rather than being confined to the borders of one nation?

■ Or, (and this is a long-standing issue) if transnational corporations are shaping the path of the global economy, what sense does it make to plan economic development on a national basis?

■ If local places are shaped and influenced by forces from around the world, why concentrate development interventions locally?

■ How can non-government organizations (NGOs) and community-based organizations (CBOs), for example, influence the development advice and inputs of globally active agencies like the World Bank and the International Monetary Fund if they remain locally focused?

[*]Diaspora is a term used to refer quite widely to communities who settle outside their homeland. Originally used of Jewish and slave diasporas, it now refers to almost any migrant community and signifies a continuing allegiance of some kind to their place of origin.

Not all of these issues are new. For much of this century, questions of local autonomy versus global dependence in relation to economic development have been important to policy-makers and communities alike. And mobility is by no means a new phenomenon, even for poor countries. Colonialism, a profoundly international set of relations, provoked movements and consolidated diasporic communities (e.g. through slavery, migrant labour or transportation) long before the emergence of large transnational firms or the idea of globalization in the late twentieth century. Nonetheless, the consequences of contemporary experiences of mobility and displacement for the practice of development are potentially substantial. Their consideration is essential if we are to contribute to reframing development to meet the challenges of the twenty-first century.

Activity 1

The focus for this Theme is the concept of 'displacement'. So far in the Introduction we have used the term to refer to a number of different processes. Take some time to re-read the Introduction so far, noting down the various ways in which the term displacement has been used. Can you identify common features across the different examples of displacement which have been mentioned so far?

In outlining what the Theme *Displacement* is all about, we have mentioned a few kinds of human displacements: *forced movements*, such as those of *refugees* or people *resettled* as a result of development projects, as well as those which are at first sight more *voluntary*, such as *rural–urban migration*, or *international migration*. All of these movements of people involve leaving one place to move to another. The term 'displacement' captures some of the significance of that movement – that people are 'displaced'; that is, they have to remove themselves from a place where they have been settled to another place. This is the most straightforward sense in which we are using the term displacement, to be able to talk about the range of difficulties and possibilities which human movements of various kinds offer for improving livelihoods and well-being. And there is a wide range, from the refugee, forced to abandon possessions and social ties, to the urban migrant, eager to seek out new opportunities.

But there is a range of related ways in which we are using the term displacement to refer to *movements of things and ideas as well*. Technological innovations have enabled the transport of goods around the world and facilitated communication between people on opposite ends of the globe. The consequences of these forms of mobility, or displacement, have been far-reaching, causing upheaval in traditional ways of life, but also representing a set of opportunities for sharing knowledge, and improving understanding.

Finally, we have noticed how *many of the borders relevant to development* through the twentieth century *have been 'displaced', undermined through flows and networks*, or *transformed* through on-going changes in the global political economy. This has vast consequences for the nature of economic activities and opportunities, for where development planning can happen, and for the possible role of local people and organizations in shaping economic change. Transnational companies may undermine national governments' development ambitions, but there are also new possibilities for *alternative forms of development* to shape both national and international agendas *through networking and alliance-building*, using the same technologies which shaped the global economy. Rather than being always bounded in nations, we need to pay attention to the emergence of relevant social, political and economic relations which can be thought of as transnational, forging connections irrespective of national borders.

Nonetheless, one of the key points which this Introduction will explore is how *territories remain important*, and how they are closely related to 'flows'. We will see how flows shape territories, and how the organization of social life around territorial divisions harnesses and directs flows, and also initiates them.

Displacement, then, is about people, things and ideas moving, and this Theme is about why this matters to development – to people who have to leave one place for another, or to economic and political agents who are able to connect one place with another.

From the discussion so far, it should also be apparent that if we are to understand these different forms of displacement and their significance, we will also need to pay careful attention to places and territories, and their meanings. The following section sets out how this Introduction will help you to develop your understanding of these concepts, and to consider why they matter to development policy and practice.

1.4 What is in this Introduction to Displacement?

Section 2 will work through some of the ways in which displacement and place have been important to development. It will elaborate on some of the points raised rather briefly in this first section, and help you to start thinking about *how places and displacements have shaped development thinking and practice.* To do this, we will look at three 'scales' of social life – the local, the national and the global. We will explore how both flows and territories have mattered to development at each of these scales, and how flows cut across these scales and transform them.

Section 3 will look in some detail at a case study of human displacement, which cuts across all three of these scales. *International human migration* involves the movement from one local area to another, across a national border, and is usually taken to be one of the key indicators of the emergence of a globally interconnected world. This section will give you an opportunity to ground your understanding of the significance of place and displacement in relation to development, in a specific empirical example.

Section 4 will take as its focus the example of *development-induced displacement* in an urban context. After considering urbanization as one important example of human displacement, this section will work through why it is that places matter to people and to development. It will specifically outline some of the dilemmas which are raised by the experience of human displacements caused through large-scale development projects, in this case an urban development scheme in Bombay/Mumbai.

By the end of this Introduction to the *Displacement* Theme, you will be able to explain why different kinds of displacement (and especially human displacements) have become important within the field of development studies, and how attention to displacement is important for a range of reasons:

- to account for development's role in causing human displacement;
- to enable more effective engagement with experiences of human displacement, some of which are forced on and devastating to individuals and communities, some of which, perhaps more voluntary, offer more of a sense of possibility; and
- to shift the focus of development studies from its association with the bounded territories of nation and locality and to reframe development so that it is more in tune with the experiences of displacement and mobility which, together with places and borders, shape contemporary social and economic life.

Summary of Section 1

1 Forced human displacements, such as refugees, are an increasing concern for humanitarian and development agencies.

2 Deliberate or intended development projects also produce many displaced people through resettlement.

3 Mobility, or displacement, of people and things is thought of as an important feature of processes of 'globalization'.

4 Development (both immanent and intended) is closely linked to movements of people and things, for example in development-induced human displacements, urbanization, or changing flows of commodities.

5 Human displacements can be both forced (as in refugees) or voluntary (as in urban migration).

6 Although mobility and displacement have become the focus of attention in much political and policy debate, there are many examples of the persistence of the significance of place and borders.

7 'Fortress Europe' exemplifies some of the barriers to human movement in an age of globalization.

8 Some borders may be less important than they once were, but new kinds of borders and places are also being put in place.

9 The empirical evidence for these changes may be disputed, but debate on these issues is changing how many aspects of social and economic life are imagined.

2 Place, displacement and development

This section will look in more detail at:

■ the importance of both displacement and place for development thinking and practice; and

■ how we can think about the *relationship* between places and experiences of displacement.

The suggestion is that development has been closely associated with specific kinds of places, or **territories**. Most important here have been the territories of the nation-state, and the local community, although more recently development has been associated with institutions and processes which operate across the entire globe. We can refer to these as different 'scales' at which human activity is organized: the local, the national and the global. Figure 2.1 is a simple diagram showing the local, national and global scales at which social and economic life has been organized. One of the key questions which we want to address in this chapter is the extent to which these scales continue to be relevant to

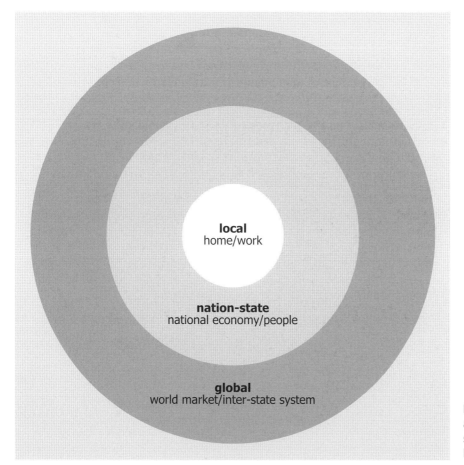

Figure 2.1 Local, national and global scales at which social and economic life has been organized.

development, as compared with the experiences of mobility and displacement outlined above, which often cut across or even seem to undermine their significance.

Territory: A clearly defined and bounded place, which is often (although not always) associated with attempts to exercise control over things and people in that place (Sack, 1985).

Territories can be identified at all sorts of scales, whether it be the home office which a parent defines as having a clear border beyond which children may not cross, or the territory of the nation-state which is governed by the rules and conventions of international law and the specific sovereign state in question. The borders around territories may seem to be very secure – the borders of states, for example, are clearly marked on the map, and the locked door of the home office may define its edges for those outside. Through this section of the Introduction, we will be thinking hard about (a) how the (always socially defined) borders around certain kinds of places, or territories, are not as impermeable as they may at first appear, and (b) how the borders which matter in social and economic life are often changing, not only their location and form, but also their meaning and significance.

2.1 Nation-states

Table 2.1 shows a range of development indicators for a selected group of African countries based on the *African Development Report 2000*. You will recall having seen tables like this at various moments in the course.

Table 2.1 Development indicators for selected African countries

Country	Population 1999 (millions)	GNP per capita 1998 (US$)	Life expectancy at birth	Adult illiteracy rate	Average annual real GDP growth rate 1991–99 (%)
Angola	12.5	350	48	n.a.	0.5
Botswana	1.6	3070	44	25	5.3
Burundi	6.6	140	43	54	−2.1
Egypt	67.2	1250	67	46	3.2
Lesotho	2.1	570	54	17	4.5
Nigeria	108.9	300	50	39	2.6
South Africa	39.9	3310	50	16	1.4
Tanzania	32.8	210	48	27	2.7
Zambia	19.0	330	41	24	1.0
Africa	**765.6**	**687**	**52**	**42**	**2.7**

Source: *African Development Report 2000* (2000), Oxford University Press for the African Development Bank.

You may find it useful to go back to *Study Guide 1* or the booklet *Preparing for Development* to refresh your memory on interpreting tables like this, and to revise some of the issues which surround the use of numerical indicators of national development. Certainly there would have been considerable differences in the accuracy and reliability of the data gathered from different countries, depending on factors such as state capacity, extant systems of data collection, date of last census and so on.

There is one feature of this data set, though, which seldom attracts critical attention. It may be so obvious that we don't stop to question it. That is that the data are presented for discrete national entities: 'Tanzania' or 'Tunisia', 'Ethiopia' or 'Lesotho'. Why should this be a problem? We are used to thinking about the world as divided up into those familiar bounded entities we call states – in fact there is no part of the world which remains formally unallocated to a state of some kind, although there are many areas where sovereignty is contested. It seems almost inevitable when we think about the range of well-being around the world that we would consider it on a country-by-country basis.

Activity 2

Take a moment to think about the calculation of development indicators on a national basis. Look back over the table of development indicators. Can you think of any reasons why the presentation of the data on a national basis might be of concern?

Comment

One clue is in the bottom line of the table, which aggregates the information for the whole of Africa. Often in popular discourse, or in the assessment of investor confidence, the continent of Africa is described as one entity. It is seen as a region which has experienced substantial economic decline, which is associated with poverty and social disorder. But if we compare the aggregate performance of all African countries with that of individual country indicators, we could find good reason to question that point of view. As the report from which the data are drawn notes:

> After showing great growth potential in the immediate post independence period, much of Africa suffered from negative per capita GDP growth for most of the four decades that followed. Africa, however, remains a region of stark contrasts and disparities country-wise and in the global context. While the continent has, in overall terms, lagged behind other regions, a few countries have produced remarkable economic results, even by world standards… . In an encouraging development, as many as 12 countries are estimated to have recorded real GDP growth rates above 5% while close to 30 countries had positive real GDP per capita growth.

> (*African Development Report 2000*, pp.xiii–1)

This example of diversity at a continental scale can help us think about the presentation of development data aggregated on a national basis. Just as there are huge variations in the indicators across different countries in Africa, we could think about the vast differences in human welfare one finds within countries – differences between the wealthiest and the poorest, between men and women, between different social and class groupings, between different regions in the country. And you will recall that there are various ways in which we can get a sense of these variations internal to countries – it is possible to disaggregate the indicators according to social groups, and it is also possible to use simple comparative indices (like Gini coefficients) to explore relative levels of inequality within as well as between countries.

However, all this is still to consider the national entities – states – as the basis for our calculations and comparisons. The point is that development – as shown by these indicators, but also more broadly – has been closely associated with the particular boundaries of states. The imagination which underpins a lot of studies of development is firmly embedded in the mosaic of states which covers the earth. Levels of development across the globe are routinely assessed on a country-by-country basis (or as larger entities, such as continents or regions, where the building blocks are still nevertheless states, as in Table 2.1) and seldom on any other basis. This is partly pragmatic – states are the sovereign entities which claim jurisdiction across territories and which routinely monopolize both the means of coercion (violence) within their borders and the powers to legislate and plan the affairs of the population in that territory (see *Introduction to Transitions*, Section 4). States are often the organizations that collect the data on which calculations about development are made.

States are also usually the entities which have the capacity to implement development plans (if not on their own, at least in association with others), or to approve or disallow certain development initiatives within their boundaries.

So, *not only do states measure and report the outcomes of immanent development, they are also closely involved in intentional development efforts* (see Chapter 2 of the Course Book for definitions of immanent and intentional development).

We can go further with this and notice that international development aid is routinely allocated on a country basis – according to the assessed need of a country, or according to the political usefulness of that country to the donor/s within their geopolitical calculations. Even capitalist investors routinely assess the suitability of investments on the basis of risk assessments or economic profiles of countries. Again this is partly for pragmatic and perfectly sensible reasons – states legislate the broader conditions in which capitalist production takes place, and shape the stability and other features of the social world in which the investor would be implicated.

There are many reasons, then, why states have come to form a central part of the development imagination. They are one of what we can call the **territorializations** of development thinking. The borders and territories of states ground much of how development studies and development practitioners often think about the world – as divided into a mosaic of states.

Territorialization: The making of territories.

Here we are thinking about how a certain delimitation, or way of cutting up the earth's surface, has been made significant in development studies. We could think counterfactually about it: Could development studies have imagined that territories described around purely language communities might have been the appropriate basis for comparing development status? Well, there are people who are very interested in language communities, especially their political importance, and who produce maps which illustrate how these groups are distributed across the earth. There may well be significant differences in development status associated with language group – think of the position of the Welsh in relation to the UK as a whole, for example. But for all the reasons above, development studies has chosen to assess development on a country-by-country basis. Although these borders already exist in the world, we are suggesting that the way of thinking about development has become territorialized or divided up, along these lines too, when we might have chosen other divisions, such as cities, or villages, or regions, or sub-continents, or (as we will consider later) flows and other kinds of cross-border interactions.

But will states continue to be the focus of development initiatives? Along with a broad disenchantment with state-led development (see Chapter 9 in the Course Book) many commentators suggest that the capacity of states to intervene in and shape economy and society within their borders has diminished substantially in the face of globalizing forces. For some states these capacities have been undermined over a long period, not only by a changing external environment, but also through a range of social and political processes which have weakened their infrastructural capacities (to shape and intervene in society). In some cases, even their ability to retain the monopoly of coercive forces (as discussed in *Introduction to Transitions*), considered a distinguishing characteristic of modern states, has been severely compromised. What some commentators call 'weak states' with a purely juridical form of statehood (in name and in law only, with little empirical ability to act as states) are unable to engage in state-directed development. This is particularly severe in some parts of Africa and South America (Leftwich, 2000).

In addition, processes of globalization or internationalization of the world economy have changed the ways in which states can shape their national economies, and according to some commentators have 'hollowed' out (or undermined) their powers. Supra-national and sub-national bodies have assumed functions or roles which nation-states used to undertake.

In the face of growing transnational investment flows and movements of people and cultural inputs, the economic and political basis of the nation-state is being substantially altered.

But it is also argued that states remain key agents in this new context; they first of all agree to transfer sovereignty to political bodies operating at other scales (global, local), and subsequently co-ordinate and manage their inter-relations. Thus although, as Hirst and Thompson (1996, p.183) put it, 'Politics is becoming more polycentric, with states as merely one level in a complex system of overlapping and often competing agencies of government', this does not mean that states have become irrelevant or insignificant in shaping the global economy.

We need to appreciate both the continuing role of states and the transnational flows which have become a significant component of the global political economy. The example of refugees perhaps highlights this best of all. Refugees are often fleeing from conflicts within states, or the actions of relatively powerful repressive states (Figure 2.2). So on the one hand, their very existence is usually bound up with state-level processes. But they are also testimony to the fact that states aren't 'hermetically closed to the outside world' (Hassner, 1998, p.277). Refugees figure prominently in the creation of transnational communities, stretching across the borders of nation-states, and the management of refugee crises has generated one of the more prominent international institutional regimes (centrally, United Nations High Commissioner for Refugees). However, controls on refugee movements speak most strongly to the continued importance of the state: 'While, on the ground, the role of international and non-governmental forces has grown enormously, the opposite happens as far as admission and exclusion are concerned: there, the role of states, and in particular of governments, is more and more decisive, not to say exclusive' (Hassner, 1998, p.277). For Hassner, refugees, and their vulnerability to the

Figure 2.2 Kosovar Albanian refugees at a camp on the Macedonia-Kosovo border having been forced to flee their homes, 1999.

decisions of nation-states as they seek safe haven in foreign countries, are a 'terrifying reaffirmation of territory, nation or state' (p.280). Citing a French geographer, Marie-Françoise Durand, he suggests that 'migration does not deterritorialize but it sharpens the tensions between territoriality and its opposite' (p.280). (We explore this paradox in greater detail in Part 2 of this Theme.)

There are many commentators, then, who stress the process of **deterritorialization** in the contemporary world, a consequence of increasing flows and movements of people, goods and ideas. Territories which might previously have been taken for granted, or thought of as natural parts of the political or economic landscape, like nation-states, come to seem less coherent and stable, and perhaps even in danger of disappearing altogether. There are more subtle conclusions, though, which suggest that flows and networks may encourage deterritorializations, but that they can also reinforce existing territorial entities (e.g. states which guard their borders more zealously) and may even support new kinds of territorializations (as in emerging supra-national and local bodies).

Deterritorialization: A broad term to refer to the ways in which socially defined territories are transformed, usually in the face of flows or changing power relations. So, the borders of nation-states, for example, become more porous in the face of 'globalization', and the state is, in certain respects, deterritorialized, as people and economic activities stretch beyond its control and sovereignty is redistributed to local and supra-national (like the EU) institutions.

Processes of **re-territorialization** might then be observed: either old territorial divisions assume new functions (states become increasingly bound up with regulating flows of people, or negotiating relations between supra-national and sub-national forms of government), or new kinds of territories become important (for example, in promoting economic investment nation-states have arguably become less powerful, but local governments have found new ways of encouraging international investment in their localities).

Development studies, as a field of intellectual and human endeavour, needs to respond to these changing geographies of the global economy. It needs to engage with questions of economic flows, transnationalization of economics, politics and culture, and also with the emergence of new kinds of territorial forms.

Another of the increasingly significant territorializations with which development studies has been associated for some time, is that of the 'local'. With the apparent decline in nation-state capacities, the scale of the local has acquired renewed importance. The following section considers this in some detail.

2.2 'Local' knowledge

At the same time as the significance of the territory of the nation-state is changing in the face of various forms of displacement, whether this be human displacement or the mobility of goods and ideas, so the scale of the local is being brought into view within development studies, for some of the same reasons. A range of processes has made the local scale much more prominent within development thinking since the 1960s, and the dominant paradigm of participatory development, as well as proponents of alternative development, give the local scale priority in their programmes for change. Development thinkers and practitioners, then, have found it important and useful to imagine a territorial entity, the 'local', which they have come to understand as a distinctive and valuable repository of knowledge and cultural practices. It is argued that for development interventions to succeed, local perspectives and local needs have to be taken into account.

Community development has a long history within the field of development – beginning with colonial programmes of social development. So it is not that the scale of the local has only just arrived on the scene – far from it. But it has certainly gained a new prominence in the face of several overlapping trends, all working to make the local a privileged site of development practice and thinking. Development practitioners don't assume the local is homogeneous, though. Many examples of development interventions have contributed to a sensitivity to differences and power relations within the sphere of the local village, community or neighbourhood. Negotiating competing interests and forms of representation and participation at the local level has become a significant component of the skills required of development planners and workers. Along with the nation-state, then, much development thought and practice has come to be territorialized around the idea of the local community.

Mohan and Stokke (2000) identify the following *four trends in development thinking and practice* which have all fostered an emphasis on the local:

1   *Decentralization.* In search of more effective forms of governance, international agencies have encouraged decentralization of the state to replace strongly centralized government structures in many poorer countries. This has usually been accompanied by a neoliberal policy agenda including the privatization of public services alongside deregulation and delegation of responsibility to lower levels of government. The role of local citizens and consumers within the system of governance has been emphasized along with more democratic forms of local government.

2   *Participatory development.* What began as a radical alternative to mainstream development has come to be a paradigm shift within

Figure 2.3 Women's collective to improve their poor housing, a participatory development project supported by UK Department for International Development, Calcutta, 1997.

development studies, as the suggestion that local knowledge and local communities are often more effective foundations for development projects than outsiders and formal scientific knowledge. More or less emphasis on local empowerment might accompany these approaches, depending on the institutions and individuals concerned (Figure 2.3).

3   *Social capital.*[*] The concept of social capital, initially formulated in a Northern context, has been extended to suggest that locally based networks of social ties, norms and trust are a significant resource for local development in poor communities, and interventions to identify and enhance these resources have become popular.

*For a definition, see the Course Book, p.37.

4   *Social movements.* Proponents of alternative development, such as Arturo Escobar and John Friedmann, draw on a participatory approach, to suggest that locally based social movements could challenge entrenched structures of power relations, promote democratization and enable more progressive forms of engagement with the state and global capital. Local social movements are considered to be privileged sites for generating new development visions.

Through the second half of the twentieth century, then, development practices have been increasingly territorialized around the scale of the 'local'.

More and more, development practitioners and thinkers advocate that any intentional development activities should pay proper attention to the complexities of a particular local context, and should especially be guided by the knowledge and concerns of local people. The following activity invites you to read an extract from one of the key thinkers in development to have advocated the importance of the local in the context of participatory development. We will then take some time to think more carefully about this scale of development activity, especially considering how 'local' places are related to 'external' forces.

Activity 3

Read the extract below which describes the practice of participatory development with its emphasis on local areas and local communities. The extract is written by Robert Chambers, one of the foremost advocates of this approach. You will also recall a discussion of his work on the *Study Guide 1* audiocassette programme 'Whose Knowledge Counts?' which you might like to review. As you read the extract, take notes about (1) the reasons Chambers offers for valuing local input and the difficulties involved in doing so; and (2) the different kinds of associations he makes with the terms 'local' and 'outsiders'. You might like to draw up a table listing the different qualities assigned to these two categories, 'local' and 'outsider'.

Paradigm shifts and the practice of participatory research and development

There are three main ways in which 'participation' is used. First, it is used as a cosmetic label, to make whatever is proposed appear good. Donor agencies and governments require participatory approaches and consultants and managers say that they will be used and then later that they have been used, while the reality has often been top-down in a traditional style. Second, it describes a co-opting practice, to mobilize local labour and reduce costs. Communities contribute their time and effort to self-help projects with some outside assistance. Often this means that 'they' (local people) participate in 'our' project. Third, it is used to describe an empowering process which enables local people to do their own analysis, to take command, to gain in confidence, and to make their own decisions. In theory, this means that 'we' participate in 'their' project, not 'they' in 'ours'. It is with this third meaning and use that we are mainly concerned here.

The paradigm shift, from things to people

The new popularity of participation has several origins: recognition that many development failures originate in attempts to impose standard top-down programmes and projects on diverse local realities where they do not fit or meet needs; concern for cost-effectiveness, recognizing that the more local people do the less that capital costs are likely to be; preoccupation with sustainability, and the insight that if local people themselves design and construct they are more likely to meet running costs and undertake maintenance; and ideologically for some development professionals, the belief that it is right that poor people should be empowered and should have more command over their lives.

The paradigm shift in practice

The shift towards empowering participation has been helped by new practices. Four stand out. First, again and again it has been found that activities it was supposed outsiders had to perform can be performed as well or better by insiders – local people, and whether literate or non-literate. This depends on outsiders encouraging them and giving them confidence that 'they can do it'. These activities include appraisal, analysis, planning, experimenting, implementing, and monitoring and evaluation. Beyond this, local people are good extensionists, and facilitators for each other's analysis. (A village volunteer has sent a note to an Aga Khan Rural Support Programme staff member in Gujarat saying – we are going to conduct a PRA* – you do not need to come). Villagers have also presented their analyses in capital cities (with PRA in Colombo, Dhaka and Gaborone). They have also begun to become trainers for non-governmental organization staff.

*PRA, participatory rural appraisal.

Second, increasingly, technologies, approaches and methods are spread laterally by peers rather than vertically through transfer of technology. Farmer-to farmer extension, both within and between countries and ecological zones, is becoming more prevalent. In PRA, the best trainer/ facilitators for other villages and other villagers are local people who have already gained experience. (The best teachers of students are also often other students, a lesson which hierarchically organized universities might do well to note and act on.)

Third, group-visual synergy refers to what often happens when a group of people engage in a visual form of analysis. Examples are mapping, scoring with seeds or counters, and making diagrams of change, trends and linkages. As groups cumulatively build up a visual representation of their knowledge, judgements and preferences, they tend to increase in commitment and enthusiasm, and to generate consensus. The outsiders observe, and can see and judge the validity of what is being shown and shared. There are opportunities to encourage and support weaker and shyer members of a community, either to join in with a group, or to form their own. Both the outsiders and the analysts find the process interesting, and often fun.

Fourth, a key element usually missing from earlier participatory efforts is the behaviour and attitudes of uppers. Empowerment of the poor requires reversals and changes of role. In PRA this has come to be recognized as more important than the methods. In consequence, much PRA training stresses how uppers behave with lowers, handing over the stick, sitting down, listening and learning, facilitating, not wagging the finger or lecturing, and being respectful and considerate. With hindsight, it is astounding that this has not been regarded as fundamental in development work, and that it is only in the 1990s that it is coming to the fore. Some of the new approaches and methods, especially of PRA, make reversals less difficult and improbable than they used to be because they are found to be effective, interesting and fun.

(Chambers, 1998, pp.30–32; 37–39)

Comment

We found Chambers' discussion of participatory development (in this brief extract and on the audiocassette) challenging and even inspiring. Pointing out the limitations of Western scientific knowledge and of remote bureaucrats deciding the futures of local communities certainly poses a challenge to many of the 'normal' ways in which state interventions and development projects have been undertaken – and failed. But in response to the first part of the activity, it would seem that there are some rather cynical ways in which participation can be used by development institutions. The prevalence of participation as simply a means to an end, or even participation that is ignored in the face of project deadlines and financial constraint, shows how very difficult it is to achieve the reversals in power relations which Chambers is advocating.

How did you do on the second part of the activity? We drew up the following table listing the qualities which Chambers associated with local people, and those he saw as characterizing outsiders. Also listed are a few of the qualities which might characterize these different groups if the existing relationships were reversed:

Local	Outsiders
Lowers	Uppers
Complex	Simplifying
Poor (and élite)	Rich
Diversity	Control
Lower class	Elite
Ignorant	Educated
Weak	Strong
Distinctive	Universalizing
REVERSALS	
Knowledgeable	Ignorant
Analysts	Observers
Speaking	Listening

In the same way as Chambers hopes for a reversal of power relations between the powerful and the poor, or what he calls uppers and lowers, he also wants to see a reversal in the prioritization of 'outside' and 'local' knowledge and interests. Now we can see already from the table above that this relationship is rather more complicated than a simple binary opposition. Consider the association of the local with both poor people and an élite. The local community is divided along many other lines as well – gender, age, perhaps ethnicity or class, caste or race. And if we think about it for a moment, the 'outside' forces which are impacting on local communities are likely to be quite divided as well. Consider the potential differences amongst governments and investors, local administrators as opposed to regionally based officials, or NGOs as opposed to agencies of international development institutions. His vision of the outsiders as initiating and encouraging processes of participation suggests that external forces of some kind remain important, even in participatory development. Chambers' vision may offer an important moral critique of the 'normal' practices of development planners, but it has come in for some criticism.

If you recall the audiocassette discussion 'Whose Knowledge Counts', you might have picked up Teddy Brett of the London School of Economics observing that external knowledge and external forces are crucial in delivering many of the fundamental requirements of poor people – roads, railways and national economic management, for example. And later on, Robert Chambers himself acknowledges that outsiders' knowledge may well be superior in relation to 'microscopic' entities (like cells and bacteria), and to knowledge of wider macro-economic forces. But he also notes that deploying these knowledges effectively in local situations still requires local support and local knowledge.

Perhaps we would do better to think of the relationship as one in which locals and outsiders are in a constant process of negotiating power relations. As Gardner and Lewis observe, 'people do not passively receive knowledge or directions from the outside, but dynamically interact with it' (1996, p.74). And they suggest that local people may choose to represent themselves to outsiders in different ways to try and extract maximum benefit out of the relationship. While well-meaning outsiders may seek to locate independent local organizations and identify local capabilities, local people may wish to present themselves as needing help, in order to ensure they capture resources which seem to be on offer. What is considered to be local reality is subject to contestation and disagreement, and as likely to change with the context as any other social phenomena might.

Mohan and Stokke (2000, pp. 254) suggest that: 'In [Chambers'] spatio-political schema the 'local' and the 'non-local' are treated as discrete entities, entirely separable from each other in space.' This offers a challenge to how we imagine the local. Far from being isolated and bounded, separate from the rest of the world (the 'outside'), Mohan and Stokke, and a number of other commentators, suggest that what is referred to as 'local' is itself the outcome of many different processes, which stretch across a variety of different scales. In this viewpoint, what we have been calling *processes of displacement are intrinsically bound up in producing local places*. The rest of this section explores what this observation means, and some of its implications.

Activity 4

Read the description below of the two remote Zambian villages of Kibala and Bukama, part of the district of Chizela (see Figure 2.4). The extract is taken from a book by Kate Crehan called *Fractured Community: Landscapes of Power and Gender in Rural Zambia* (1997). As you read, make a note of the range of processes shaping the fortunes of the villages over time. To what extent would you consider these processes to be local, and to what extent would you assume that they originated outside the villages?

> Both Kibala and Bukama are located in the heart of the region associated with the Kaonde people which stretches over much of Zambia's North-Western Province, and both were seen locally as clearly Kaonde communities in which a Kaonde way of life was followed. The large majority of their inhabitants defined themselves to me as Kaonde, Kaonde was the language normally spoken, even by the non-Kaondes, and it was

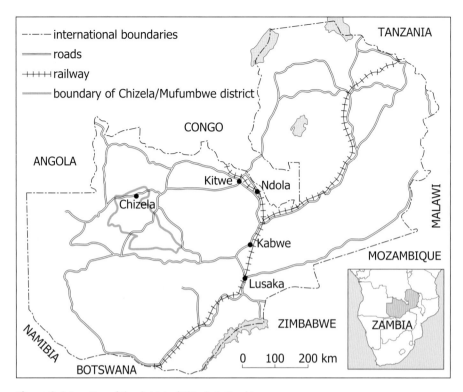

international boundaries
roads
railway
boundary of Chizela/Mufumbwe district

TANZANIA
CONGO
ANGOLA
Kitwe · Ndola
Chizela
Kabwe
MALAWI
MOZAMBIQUE
Lusaka
ZIMBABWE
ZAMBIA
NAMIBIA
BOTSWANA
0   100   200 km

Figure 2.4 Location of the district of Chizela in Zambia.

Kaonde chiefs who were described as 'owners' of the area. The all-important kinship links, which, in local eyes, were what provided a community with its basic armature, were dominated by the Kaonde matrilineal pattern of descent. According to Kaonde kinship rules, a child belongs to its mother's clan, and marriage is forbidden within the matrilineal clan...

The histories of the two communities were very different. Kibala was a long-established cluster of approximately thirty small settlements, crosscut by a dense network of kinship ties, with a population of close to 800 in 1988 and its own chief, Chief Kibala. Indeed, the people of Kibala maintained that in the late nineteenth century, at the time the region first came under the control of the British South African Company (BSAC), the Kibala chiefdom had been one of the most important Kaonde chiefdoms and that it was at the time senior to that of Chizela. Its importance, however, declined during the colonial period, and in 1944 the colonial government ceased to recognize it as a separate chiefdom, amalgamating it into that of Chizela. To the people of Kibala, however, and to many other local Kaonde, Chief Kibala was still a chief.

The people of Kibala produced relatively little in the way of crops for sale. Chizela District, like much of the region associated with the Kaonde, was a tsetse-infected area, and in 1988 cultivation was still for the most part a hoe-based, slash-and-burn cultivation system. This pattern of shifting cultivation (often referred to throughout Zambia by the term for the Bemba variant, *citimene*) has a long history of being condemned by both colonial and postcolonial governments; only the degree of condemnation, and the reasons given for why *citimene* was wrong, seem to have varied over the years. At the heart of the Kaonde cultivation system, at least according to local ideology, was the cultivation of sorghum. Central to the idea of Kaonde identity, both when Kaonde people were describing themselves and when they were described by their neighbours, was that they were 'sorghum eaters'. 'Being Kaonde' meant eating *nshima* (the solid porridge that constitutes the staple food throughout Zambia) made from sorghum rather than maize, millet or cassava. In fact in the 1980s what people actually ate in Chizela was often maize, not sorghum, but in terms of ideology sorghum was still considered to be the 'real' Kaonde staple. ... The practice of shifting cultivation meant that the villages of Kibala had occupied many different sites over the years. The core meaning of the Kaonde term for village, '*muzhi*' (plural *mizhi*), was not, however, a particular place but a particular kinship group, and as kinship groups many of the *mizhi* that made up Kibala were perceived as entities with histories stretching back into the pre-colonial period.

Bukama's origins were far more recent than Kibala's. It was established as a farm settlement in 1977 as part of a Dutch-funded development project. The idea was to encourage 'progressive' farming by providing properly 'motivated' individuals with ten-hectare (approx. twenty-five acre) plots in an area of relatively good soil on which they were supposed to grow some crops for their own subsistence but also maize and other crops for sale to the national marketing board. In the years since the scheme's founding the numbers of registered plot holders had fluctuated, reaching 40 at its peak, but never achieving the numbers planned by the scheme's architects and declining to 34 (of whom 12 were women) by 1988. ...

The architects of the Bukama scheme, like those of many other similar schemes, believed that concentrating 'progressive' farmers in this way would have the twin advantages of freeing them from what were seen as the constraints of 'traditional' communities and of making it easier and cheaper to provide them with the various services they would need for 'modern' farming, such as the provision of inputs, extension services, and marketing facilities. By the late 1980s, though, the promised tractor services had ceased to materialize and few people were cultivating a significantly larger area than those in neighbouring areas outside the scheme. ... All those who had settled on the scheme came from relatively close by, and even though there was not the same density of crosscutting kin ties, virtually all those living there had some kinship links with others in Bukama.

The composition of the Bukama settlement did differ significantly from that of Kibala, however, in that there was a far higher percentage of female-headed households, 35 percent as against 12 percent. In reality, whatever the intentions of those who had devised Bukama, many of those who had moved there had done so at the suggestion of Chief Chizela; and why he had suggested it was usually because there had been some dispute (often involving an accusation of witchcraft) that he had sought to resolve by encouraging one of the parties to move to Bukama. As a result Bukama had something of a reputation as a place full of troublemakers and witches. The significance of this, however, should not be overestimated given that ... accusations of witchcraft were omnipresent in both Kibala and Bukama. What is true is that Bukama had attracted a number of people, including a disproportionate number of widows and divorced women, who had found their previous villages less than hospitable.

(Crehan, 1997, pp.3–5)

Comment

My list of external forces at work in these villages was as follows:

Pre-colonial trade and social relations with neighbouring and distant communities

BSAC (British South Africa Company)

Colonial government

Post-colonial government – policies, officials, services

Urban employers

Foreign donors

From reading the rest of Kate Crehan's book, from which this extract was taken, we are also aware that missionaries, traders, and immigrants from neighbouring countries have also helped to shape the area. External forces have been at work in this corner of Zambia for all of recorded human history. It is thought that the current inhabitants, for example, moved there over a century ago from areas further north. Nonetheless, a strong sense of local identity can still be identified.

In the extract, Kate Crehan suggests that the community, mostly Kaonde people, have a strong sense of their identity – partly reflected in the distinctive food they preferred to eat. This suggests a long historical process of differentiating themselves from other, possibly neighbouring groups, who might have different traditions. Later on in the book, she discusses how this sense of a local Kaonde identity was also facilitated by missionaries writing down the language and in that way defining the group as distinct from neighbouring communities. In the first part of the century the British South Africa Company was responsible for administering the area and, finding it lacking in mineral resources, recruited labourers to work on mines in other parts of the wider region, in Zimbabwe, Tanzania and South Africa as well as in Zambia. And the gender balance in the villages of Kibala and Bukama still reflects the long tradition of men (and some women) moving to find work in towns and mines for at least part of their lives.

Colonial and post-colonial governments have sought to influence settlement patterns, farming habits and the political organization of the region. But Crehan provides a lot of rich ethnographic material to explore how the kinship-based social relations of the villagers and the chief were intertwined in complex ways with those of government. In the extract she discusses how local chiefly interventions in disputes over witchcraft meshed with state and donor strategies to modernize agriculture to shape the locality of Bukama. Local people were not simply drawn along passively in the wake of these forces. Rather, 'outsiders' were interpreted, assessed and engaged with selectively on the basis of the changing economic needs and social judgements of local people.

Even such a short description of one of the more remote areas of a very poor country demonstrates that what is 'local' is very much a product of wider forces. This does not make the place any less local! Rather, the distinctive qualities of one place are at least partly the outcome of diverse (external) forces which operate at a range of scales – some more restricted to the locality or region, but some, such as trading links with foreign countries, which can stretch across the globe. And we can also appreciate that what might at first sight seem like an external force – 'government in Lusaka', for example – is shaped and influenced by the interests and concerns of people in these villages.

Local dynamics and wider social forces interact to produce the distinctive histories and experiences of particular places.

Although the region had experienced a lot of out-migration to urban areas and mines, and had in this sense experienced physical 'displacements', people living in the villages of Kibala and Bukama have been part of a wide range of social processes for a very long time. There are two important things to note in relation to this. Firstly, that remaining put in a local area does not mean that global forces are irrelevant – 'displacement' in the form of significant social and economic change can well be experienced in a local place without going anywhere. Secondly, that these places cannot be thought of as separate from external or global forces. In fact, and following Mohan and Stokke's criticism of Chambers, we need to think carefully about whether it is helpful to make such a firm distinction between 'local' and 'external' forces.

In a case study of local agricultural change in an Indian village called Alipur, Akhil Gupta notes that local farmers are as willing to either draw upon or reject 'local' knowledge as they are 'Western' knowledge. Both were equally a part of their understandings and agricultural practices:

> Farmers were as likely to draw on – and contest – hegemonic (Western or national) meanings of development as they were to employ – and resist – dominant (that is, indigenous) understandings of agriculture. Was there, then, any good reason to regard discourses of development as 'external' and indigenous knowledges of agronomy as 'internal' to the lives of the inhabitants of Alipur?

(Gupta, 1998, p.6)

Gupta raises an important issue about 'local knowledge', which, as we have seen in the Zambian case study, is likely to have been constituted over time through a vast range of links and networks of relations stretching beyond the bounds of the village. If the 'local' is indeed the outcome of social relations stretched across various scales, then it would be appropriate in the case of the Indian village just mentioned to see the specific local combination of understandings about agricultural production there as a result older ideas and more recent, supposedly Western, versions of 'development' of both.

Activity 5

Return to the table you drew up in Activity 3 to summarize Chamber's views of the contrasts between local and outside forces. Can you think of how you might revise this in the light of the discussion so far?

Comment

I would probably start again! It might be better to list some of the features of the local which had emerged from the Zambian example, and think about external forces in relation to the local, rather than as quite separate from local realities. See if you can add to this list.

Local places are:	External forces are:
Distinctive	Changed by local activities
Divided	Located in places
Dynamic	Contested
A product of various external forces	
Linked to wider networks	
Shaping outsider's agendas	

Doreen Massey (1995) has called this way of thinking about place a 'global sense of place'. *Far from being counterposed to external forces, the local is made up of those forces*, and processes which seem to be 'external' are very much a part of, as well as shaped and produced in, particular places. These may seem like complex and abstract points: do they make a difference to development thinking and practice?

As we noted at the beginning of this section, development practice has become heavily invested in local participatory methods of intervention in communities based on an appreciation of local or indigenous knowledge and capacities. *An understanding of some of the dynamics by which local communities are produced could be helpful to support effective development interventions or community-based initiatives.*

Much has been written about the importance of recognizing that local 'communities' are far from homogeneous entities, and are often internally divided (e.g. by gender, race, class, caste) and shaped by a range of different power relations. Some of the divisions within communities are produced and shaped through the wider social relations we have been discussing. This might involve people who have successfully harnessed external resources to personal advantage (like state positions, development aid, or economic flows). Alternatively, some people might find their concerns diverging from fellow residents as a result of changing experiences, ideas or beliefs. Perhaps most obviously, 'local' people move, travel and have their own networks of links beyond their home, all of which can shape their personal futures and the development of the locality.

Attempting to build only on 'local' knowledge might neglect some key elements of the resourcefulness of local people which are drawn from beyond the apparent boundaries of the locality. In relation to social capital, for example, far from being purely local, some writers have shown that 'thickening' or increasing social capital often depends on interventions from external agents, such as the state, NGOs, churches and international allies. Jonathan Fox (1996) describes the celebrated Mexican example of the Zapatistas, who built on church organizations, state reforms and international allies to thicken social capital and enhance their political campaigns. On the other hand, creating a strong sense of locality might be a crucial strategy for gaining access to resources, as in examples of effective community mobilization and protest. Unfortunately, external forces are not always potential resources; there are also many ways in which they can impact negatively on local communities, such as through rising prices of commodities or decreases in state services.

In the field of *alternative development*, the importance of understanding the interaction between the 'local' and the 'global' has come to the fore as ways of challenging wider structures of power and inequality have been sought. John Friedmann notes, for example, that 'Although alternative development must begin locally, it cannot end there' (1992, p.7). He explains this a little more in the preface to his book *Empowerment* (see chapter 1 of the Course Book for a discussion of his approach):

> The empowerment approach, which is fundamental to an alternative development, places the emphasis on autonomy in the decision-making of territorially organized communities, local self-reliance (but not autarchy), direct (participatory) democracy, and experiential social learning. Its starting point is the locality, because civil society is most readily mobilised around local issues. But local action is severely constrained by global economic forces, structures of unequal wealth, and hostile class alliances. Unless these are changed as well, alternative development can never be more than a holding action to keep the poor from even greater misery and to deter the further devastation of nature. If an alternative development looks to the mobilization of civil society at the grass roots or, as Latin Americans like to say, in communities 'at the base', it must also, as a second and concurrent step, seek to transform social into political power and to engage the struggle for emancipation on a larger – national and international – terrain.
>
> (Friedmann, 1992, pp.vii–viii)

There has been much concern within this approach with how myriad local movements, locally based NGOs and local initiatives can be 'scaled up' to challenge global forces. For example, Holland and Blackburn (1998) note the challenges of 'amplifying the voice of the poor' through drawing participatory research methods, such as those advocated by Robert Chambers, into nation-wide policy-making. Also the possibilities of encouraging NGO networking to challenge global development institutions, or of building global social movement alliances, are being actively explored. Friedmann's argument is that local initiatives and national and global forces need to be drawn into relationship with one another, and to mutually transform each other, if alternative development is to become a reality. (We explore this in some detail in Part 2 of this Theme.)

This is an advance on Chambers' thinking about local and external forces as separate spheres, but it still does not draw on the idea that local and external forces have already shaped each other, which we observed in the case of the Zambian villages (Activity 4). Rather than there being a 'quantum leap from the local to the global' (Friedmann, 1992, p.31), we could argue that the local and the global are already closely intertwined. Does this hold out more hope for the emergence of an alternative development? Clearly, whether local or global, inequality and imbalances in power remain to limit the potential for change in the circumstances of poorer people everywhere. But the idea that some positive local forces have already shaped wider social relations, and that they have the potential to do this in the future, might make one more optimistic about the emergence of alternative development. Perhaps elements of it are already with us?

Even as the local has been identified as a significant field of development activity, debates about the role of external interventions in the sphere of the local direct us towards a set of processes which seem to be of much wider scope than the borders of the local. Through the 1980s and 1990s, there has been a tendency to contrast the 'local' with 'global' forces of operation – although there has also been much controversy about the nature of the relationship between these two 'scales'. Before turning in Section 3 to examine in more detail the dynamic relations between global processes and local places through the example of human migration, let us consider first how development thinking and practice has also been organized around the idea and phenomenon of the global.

2.3 Global imperatives

At quite the other end of the scale of human activity from local development, debates are increasingly being shaped by yet another 'territorialization' – the idea of the 'global'. While local initiatives are valued and encouraged, there is a strong sense that there is a set of forces ranged against the territories of the 'local' and the 'state' which perhaps threaten their potential development, or for some (more hopefully) offer a set of opportunities for future growth and improvements in welfare. But most commentators are agreed that something called the 'global' is an inevitable component of development ambitions at whatever scale, and certainly a major force in shaping 'immanent' development.

Activity 6

You should take some time now to review your notes on the arguments presented in Chapter 16 of the Course Book, 'Sustainable globalization?', where Anthony McGrew discusses globalization at some length. Take particular note of pp.345–359. As you do so, draw together your understandings of globalization around the following key questions:

- define globalization for yourself;
- identify some of the kinds of flows that make up globalization;
- identify some of the agents responsible for shaping globalization;
- think about where globalization is produced or influenced from.

Comment

We found McGrew's summary definition in Box 16.1 (Course Book, p.347) very helpful in keeping clearly in mind what globalization entails. As he puts it, it involves the 'widening scope, deepening impact and speeding up of *inter-regional flows and networks of interaction* within all realms of social activity from the cultural to the criminal.'

We've added italics to the quote to highlight what we think is one of the crucial points about globalization, certainly for the arguments and concerns of this Theme. This is that it involves new kinds of flows and networks around the world, new both in terms of quantity (there is an increasing number of links) and quality (there is a deepening, speeding up, and widening of these links).

We will explore this aspect of globalization as flows and networks in more detail in the following section, where we will consider human migration in some detail. For the moment, it is important to notice in McGrew's discussion that these flows involve very specific movements, from one place to another. They take on a wide variety of different forms and connect different parts of the world, depending on the nature of the flow or connection involved. In sum, 'globalization' is not something 'out there' but is a shorthand for a complex set of diverse social interactions and movements across the globe, which are changing in related ways, often due to technological innovation and the reorganization of the global economy (see the box on p.348 on what is driving globalization).

McGrew goes on to make some important points about how the 'global' economy and society are organized. The key point here is that *globalization is uneven, unequal and shaped by power relations*. There are some agents shaping the global economy who are more powerful than others: international agencies such as the International Monetary Fund, or richer countries who have more power to set the rules for trade and engagement. But this is not to suggest that other agents, in poorer countries, or those who are disadvantaged by, or even excluded from globalization, do not shape globalization. The politics of the global political economy is highly contested, both by nations and by popular and transnational organizations 'from below' – as envisaged by the advocates of alternative development. The flows and networks that make up what we call the global, and how they can and should be regulated or influenced are subject to fierce political contestation.

Nonetheless, McGrew points out that the power relations of globalization are uneven: 'the key sites of global power ... are, quite literally, oceans apart from the communities whose destiny they shape' (p.348). Thus, on the one hand, globalization has created what McGrew calls *a 'more fluid or pluralistic' form of global politics*, with nation-states joined by regional organizations, international regulatory agencies and inter-governmental organizations, transnational political movements and international NGOs in the field of politics. By contrast, there have been some strong polarizations of power relations in different institutions and localities – consider the location of the White House and the World Bank in Washington, for example, or the headquarters of major transnational corporations and finance houses in New York. Both involve significant *localizations of global power*, which may facilitate the exercise of power across the globe; but they also provide opportunities for concentrating opposition to powerful global forces in these places (Chambers, 1998).

In 1999/2000, for example, a series of globally-co-ordinated protests against international agencies grabbed the world's attention. Running battles with police outside the World Trade Organization negotiations in Seattle in late November 1999 characterized one of many protests during this period which brought together activists from around the globe, finding common purpose in their opposition to the impacts of globalization from above and at the G8 meeting in Genoa in July 2001. Protests outside the World Bank in Washington in April 2000 again highlighted the significance of certain concentrations of global power for enabling protest movements to focus their opposition.

Nonetheless, *accompanying the transnationalization of politics and economic activity has been the reinforcing of older boundaries and divisions*, such as that of the nation-state (see p.359 of the Course Book). The implications of this changing architecture of the world order for development are substantial – both in terms of *deterritorializations* consequent upon flows, and in terms of *re-territorializations* around reconfigured states and localities, and new kinds of regionalizations.

Firstly, McGrew notes that as well as reconfiguring the architecture, or geography, of politics, the geography of poverty across the world is changing with the current phase of globalization. No longer easily assigned to a 'Third World' or the 'South', McGrew suggests that concentrations of poverty – and consequently many of the concerns of development – now stretch across former first and third world divisions. The increasing entwining of the fortunes of all countries within the realm of the global reinforces his point that *development is increasingly a 'shared concern' of all countries*, and that globalization has been responsible for 'reconfiguring both the agenda and the politics of development' (p.355).

It is this suggestion, that development as practice and as a body of thought has had to reconsider aspects of its understandings and activities in the wake of the substantial transformations in the architecture of the global world order, that has motivated this Theme.

The specific focus of the Theme will be on one of the central defining features of globalization: inter-regional flows and networks, or what we have chosen to term 'displacements'.

It is a striking feature of the changing geography of the global political economy that these flows and networks seem to cut across and transform, or perhaps displace, some of the long-standing elements of global politics and economics: nations, localities and the structure of international relations based on a system of states. At times it seems these structures are undermined, at others they seem to be transformed or even reinforced. McGrew discusses the emergence of the 'activist state' on p.359, for example, where globalization has stimulated a range of new strategic responses on the part of some nation-states to shape economic growth, rather than leading everywhere to the demise of state capacities for intervention in the economy.

These territorializations (the local, the national, the global) and the various displacements causing deterritorialization have important consequences for development thinking and practice. The dynamics and politics of globalization have raised substantial questions about how territorial entities like local communities and the state fare in the face of the increasing significance of flows and networks in social and economic life. If development is to confront the challenges of globalization, as McGrew suggests, then it will need to consider what difference this new 'architecture' or geography of the global political economy – its diverse flows and networks – will make to its practices, especially insofar as they have previously been attached to territorial entities like states, systems of states, and localities. In Part 2 of this Theme, we will argue that *new kinds of agents of development* are emerging, operating through the flows and networks which comprise globalization.

The following section considers the experience of human migration. Human migration is one of the exemplary 'flows' shaping contemporary social life – many commentators consider migration to be one of the most significant indicators of the emergence of a global economy and society. Migration cuts across all three of the territorializations we have been discussing. It draws us to consider the question of the relationship between flows and territories (or place and displacement) in more detail. Although a 'flow' (of people), migration starts off in and affects local places, it is strongly influenced by national state policies, and follows certain very specific routes from one place to another. Just as places and territories (like the villages of Kibala and Bukama in Zambia) are shaped by wider processes and flows, we will suggest that flows are in turn shaped by places and territories.

Summary of Section 2

1 Development thinking and practice have been closely associated with the territorializations of the local, the state and the global.

2 Most often, development indicators and polices are articulated for national territories.

3 Although nation-states may be being 'hollowed out' in an era of globalization, they remain important actors in the international political and economic arena.

4 Various trends in development thinking and practice have made the local scale an increasingly important focus of development activity. These include: decentralization, democratization, participation and social capital.

5 Participatory methods have stressed the contrast between locals and outsiders and sought to reverse the power relations involved.

6 But localities are also a product of external influences – local and outside forces are mutually shaping of each other. We could call this a 'global sense of place'.

7 Empowerment approaches stress the need to expand political action for alternative development beyond the local.

8 Globalization, the widening and deepening of international flows and networks, cuts across and potentially transforms the territorializations of the local and the state with consequences for how development is thought and practised.

3 Global flows: the case of human migration

The example of human migration, one of the many different kinds of networks and flows which make up 'globalization', poses some valuable questions for us. First of all, it raises the issue of how place and displacement are related. Or, put another way, how flows and local places are bound up with one another. If flows are about deterritorializing social relations, then have they made territories, such as local areas, or states, irrelevant? As we have seen in the previous section, when we looked at three different scales or territorializations of development, places and displacements are very much bound up with one another: local areas are shaped by wider flows and connections, and states are being transformed by wider economic and political relations. As we turn now to look directly at one kind of 'flow' – human movements – we will be able to assess whether this conclusion still holds when we look at it from the other direction:

Q Are flows shaped by territories, just as we have seen that territories or places are shaped by flows?

And by looking directly at an example of a flow, or displacement, we can start to get a sense of how development thinking and practice might be adjusting to a world as much shaped by displacement as by the more familiar territories of states and localities. Finally, by exploring a specifically human movement, as opposed to a flow of things or ideas, we can also start to understand how and why places, or being displaced, might matter to people, insofar as they make a difference to social life, political processes, or economic well-being. We will be exploring this in more detail, though, in the final section of this Introduction, when we consider development-induced displacements.

3.1 The 'age of migration'?

There has been a lot of debate about whether or not the late twentieth century and early part of the twenty-first has seen a substantial rise in international migration, and a growth in its significance. In their survey of the history of global migration Castles and Miller (1993) observe that:

> ...international migration is a constant, not an aberration, in human history. Population movements have always accompanied demographic growth, technological change, political conflict and warfare. Over the last five centuries mass migrations have played a major role in colonialism, industrialization, the emergence of nation-states and the development of the capitalist world market. However, international migration has never been as pervasive, nor as socio-economically and politically significant, as it is today.
>
> (Castles and Miller, 1993, p.260)

By contrast, Hirst and Thompson (1996) in their book *Globalization in Question* observe that the mass migrations of the nineteenth and early twentieth century have been replaced by much smaller flows of temporary and guest workers, skilled migrants or those with family already in the country of destination (p.23). Nonetheless, Morawska and Spohn suggest that in 1992, the number of Europeans 'on the move', i.e. within and beyond Europe (excluding the much larger number of international tourists), exceeded by two to three times the numbers moving at the height of the earlier wave of migrations at the turn of the twentieth century (Morawska and Spohn, 1997, p.27). The evidence for a diverse global phenomenon like migration is truly difficult to weigh, and we have little space here to go into all the details. But it seems that most commentators agree that migration has been important for a long time, that it has changed over time (primarily from migrations for settlement, to more temporary movements and repeat journeys, often known as sojourning), and that the variety of international migrations which we can identify today are politically and socially significant.

We should also bear in mind that one's assessment of the migration situation might also be quite different depending on where you are looking from (see the discussion of standpoint in Section 10 of *Study Guide 1*). If we consider the point of view of Europe, migration is a hotly contested issue, and very closely controlled by defensive states – although both economic migrants and refugees continue to make determined (and often very expensive) efforts to penetrate Fortress Europe. So from this point of view it may seem that the age of migration is almost over, especially compared with the huge out-migrations of colonial times, and the large labour in-migrations of the post-Second World War period. Similarly, with the USA, the mass family migrations of the pre-First World War period have not been sustained.

However, if we cast our attention to the continent of Africa, we might assess the relative significance of international migration quite differently. Historically, there is much written and known about the millions of African people who were forcibly moved to the Americas in the days of the Atlantic slave trade. But it is less well known that there was a similar, and largely unrecorded, movement of African people as part of Arabic and Indian Ocean slave and other migrations (Curtin, 1997). In the contemporary period, with over half of all the world's refugees in Africa, and many porous borders between states, as well as substantial population outflows to former colonial powers, international migration may be still considered a very significant feature of life on the continent.

In post-apartheid South Africa, for example, the formal mining-related migrant labour flows of the apartheid era (at a maximum in the 1960s at around 600 000) and the historically tiny flows of Europeans, largely from the United Kingdom, have slowed down considerably or stopped. But the rise in the number of unrecorded migrants and refugees from other African countries (whether short term, circular or more permanent) has become a major political challenge for the African National Congress government. The government estimates unrecorded immigrants from Africa to be between 2 million and 10 million, a sizeable proportion of the national population (around 46 million). Post-apartheid development, some fear, is jeopardized by the increased burden these migrants place on already stretched government services and housing provision, although there is also evidence that migrants stimulate the economy, and that most do not plan to settle permanently in South Africa (Crush and Veriava, 1998) (see Box 3.1).

Box 3.1 Reviled foreign street traders declared good for the economy

by Adrian Hadland, *Sunday Independent*, 3 May 1998

Nine months ago, Ahmed Kulmiye boarded a ship in Somalia bound for Cape Town. The civil strife and feuding warlords had made life intolerable for the 24-year-old.

Educated and ambitious, Kulmiye decided to visit his brother, work as an informal trader in South Africa and save money for the return home when, he hopes, things will have calmed down.

Kulmiye is one of dozens of Somalis who have set up stalls on street corners around Cape Town, while thousands of more informal traders, from southern Africa and beyond, hawk their wares in virtually every town and city. Their reception has not always been welcoming. In August last year, protests against foreign traders erupted into violence in Johannesburg. The locals vented their anger at the foreigners for 'infesting the city streets and killing our businesses'.

But recent research suggests that informal traders in South Africa are far from a scourge and, in fact, make a genuine contribution to the economies of their home countries as well as to that of South Africa.

In a report by the Southern African Migration Project, called *Trading Places: Cross-Border Traders and the South African Informal Sector*, much of the conventional wisdom about the sector is contradicted or challenged.

According to the report, published with Idasa, almost a quarter of foreign traders employ South Africans in their operations, and very few enter South Africa without goods to sell, mostly curios and wood and stone carvings.

Almost 80 percent of traders from Southern African Development Community [SADC] countries export South African-made goods such as electronics, appliances, clothes, shoes and household goods, while half spend more than half their income in South Africa.

Other 'myths' surrounding informal traders, which the report's findings contradict, include the misconceptions that participants are poorly

---

educated or illiterate, that they are poverty-stricken and desperate, that many want to live permanently in South Africa, and that they are here illegally.

Business is brisk at Kulmiye's stall, just across from parliament. Passers-by stop to pick up sweets or cigarettes. 'I'll be home in two or three years,' he says, showing his permit. 'Then I will take money and things for my family.'

The report calls for measures to stimulate the informal economy and strengthen ties, particularly with SADC countries. It urges the government to introduce a new, temporary permit category for individual, informal cross-border traders. The permit would allow multiple re-entry, thereby lessening the chance of bribery at border posts.

The report also argues for a duty-free allowance to be assigned to goods carried by informal traders and that reciprocal arrangements should be negotiated with neighbouring countries. It calls too for the government to assist in accounting and marketing training, and to provide start-up capital.

It adds that these policy recommendations, some of which are included in a pending but delayed green paper on international migration, would build trade links, create jobs and stimulate the South African economy.

Figure 3.1 Tibetan refugee recently arrived at a Tibetan house in Kathmandu, after escaping over the Himalayas from Chinese-occupied Tibet, 1997.

The politics of migration may vary from place to place (Figure 3.1), and commentators may disagree about its numerical significance, but the contemporary experience of human mobility in the context of relatively easy telecommunications links between places, has made a difference to how people today imagine their sense of belonging, political affiliations, and opportunities for making a living. Whatever the quantitative evidence (and it is much debated), the qualitative significance of international migration, both politically and socially, remains important. We may be well advised to consider also the broader social consequences of migration experiences for different places, even if they involve relatively few people moving – as the case of European migration to South Africa, or even Australia, suggests.

Bearing in mind these contestations and differences of opinion, let us try and piece together a picture of the last few centuries of international migration, before turning to consider a specific example of movement from one region of Bangladesh to London.

Activity 7

Examine Figure 3.2 (parts a and b), which offers a visual representation of some of the major migratory flows before the Second World War (from Castles and Miller, 1993). (Note that the arrows on these maps are not drawn to scale so they do not accurately represent the size of population flows.) As you examine the maps, *consider the different social forces which might have played a role in shaping migration*. You might like to come back to the maps and review your thoughts on why these movements took place as you read through the following sections.

Note: There is not a lot of discussion in the Course Book on migration, but if you look in the index you will see a few short references to migration which might give you some ideas about this. Page 129 of the Course Book offers a brief summary of major aspects of global migration this century, for example. And you could look up references to specific forms of human movement such as slavery, indentured labour, or forced labour.

(Comments on this activity are included in the section 'International migration before 1945' below)

While the contemporary period of globalization is one in which international migration is at least as pervasive and socio-economically and politically significant as it has ever been in the past, international movements of people have also been an outstanding feature of some earlier historical periods. As with other kinds of flows which characterize the global economy, human movements have changed over time in terms of their direction, extent and meaning, with significant consequences for states and localities. The following discussion is fairly Euro-centric, and could be extended considerably with reference to the diverse histories of migrations in different parts of the world. For the moment, though, it is helpful to use the limited range of examples we can explore here to illustrate two key points:

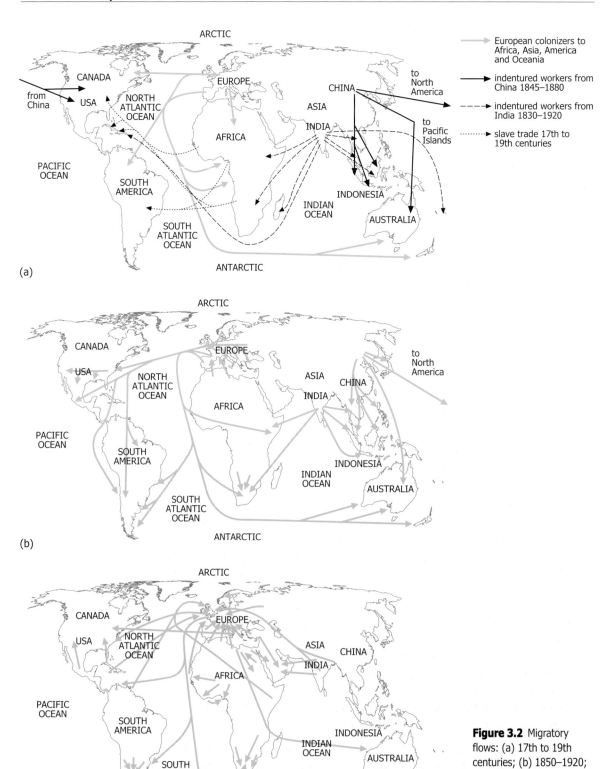

Figure 3.2 Migratory flows: (a) 17th to 19th centuries; (b) 1850–1920; (c) 1945–73. Arrow dimensions do not indicate size of movements.

Q How have migration flows both been shaped by and shaped states?

Q How is human migration related to development?

International migration before 1945

Both political and economic factors have played an important role in the nature and direction of migration flows for centuries. We can see from Figure 3.2(a) that during the period of European colonial dominance of the globe, substantial flows of people moved to new colonies and settlements from Europe. Very often these moves were attempts to escape the effects of industrialization and urbanization, or to seek new opportunities, so they might broadly be thought of as economic. But they were deeply dependent on the political control of new areas, and were also a consequence of controls over unemployed and poor people in places like the United Kingdom, where poor laws and unlegislated conditions of industrial production made the prospects of independent settlement attractive. Transportation of convicts to Australia contributed to part of the flows of unfree labour, or forced migration. But by the far the bulk of forced migration occurred as a result of the slave trade* – some 15 million slaves were estimated to have been transported from Africa to the Americas before 1850. Indentured labourers* too, whose conditions of employment and transport were technically voluntary, but at times no better than slavery, made up a large proportion of human migration – over 30 million people from the Indian sub-continent were transported around the British and Dutch colonies as indentured labourers (Castles and Miller, 1993, p.49).

*Chapter 11 of the Course Book discusses both slavery and indentured labour at some length.

While these forced migrations were closely bound up with the political system of colonialism, they were themselves lucrative trades, as slaves became commodities, and were essentially providing labour for the extensive development of trade in a range of commodities in the colonies and the Americas. *Economic and political forces worked hand in hand to shape these displacements*. Migration to Europe remained largely intra-European and mostly related to industrial and agricultural labour needs, until the post-Second World War period, although restrictive policies against certain refugee populations (e.g. Jews in the United Kingdom) and foreign workers (e.g. Poles in Germany) around the turn of the twentieth century laid the foundations for the form of late twentieth century anti-immigrant sentiment and legislation. Migration to the USA and Australia from Europe and South America, primarily, involved many millions of families and workers (see Figure 3.2b).

The period between 1918 and 1945 was one of slow economic growth and increasing hostility to immigrants in European countries and the USA. After the era of mass migration from 1850 to 1914, the inter-war period saw a considerable decline in migration (Castles and Miller, 1993, p.61).

International migration since 1945

With the post-war economic boom in advanced industrial nations, the demand for labour saw the *recruitment of workers from around the world*, very often following former colonial links or from the European periphery under the guestworker system (as shown in Figure 3.2c). Migration patterns therefore changed considerably, and the flows of people moving increased in volume once again. Migration continued under changing immigration regulations (encouraging family reunion), to the United States and Australia (Castles and Miller, 1993, p.66).

With the onset of world recession in 1973, migration patterns once more shifted. The restructuring of capitalist production in advanced industrial countries meant that labour demands were no longer so important, and the organized recruitment of labourers from former colonies and other parts of the world ceased. *Restrictive immigration legislation* saw the end of more informal migrations following established colonial links, and family reunion and the formation of new ethnic communities in Western countries characterized migration from former colonies in this period. Economic migration to the US and Australia continued, but most migrants no longer came predominantly from Europe but increasingly from South and South-east Asia and Eastern Europe. Large labour migrations from around Asia have been encouraged by oil-producing countries and new regional migrations have been stimulated by economic development in newly industrializing countries. There has also been a mass movement of refugees and asylum seekers in the period, and a tightening of immigration controls by western countries primarily in response to these movements, not only from the 'South' but also as a result of the break-up of the Soviet bloc and wars in the Balkans. *The patterns of international migration are becoming more regionalized*, as movements to neighbouring countries in different regions of the globe have become increasingly significant.

In East and South-east Asia, for example, after the mass migrations of the colonial period, which saw Indian and Chinese settlements established in many Asian countries, much of the more recent migrations in the region have been for shorter-term unskilled work, or longer-term movements of skilled workers. Asian people have recently made up about 40% of migrants to the USA and a number of governments in the region have consciously encouraged investment and worker migration to other countries in the region. The social and economic consequences of an emerging Chinese 'diaspora', with transnational business and family ties, rather than a straightforward migration from one place to another, is increasingly seen to be symptomatic of contemporary migration. More about sojourning, or shorter term labour migrations, than about permanent settlement, the experience of living and working across national territories reflects something of a qualitative shift in the meaning of migration, beyond the European-influenced model of settlement which has often shaped understandings of the experience of migration. Some commentators trace these changes to the increased ease of communication and travel, broadly associated with processes of 'globalization'.

Transnational communities and migrant workers often continue to play an important role in the social and economic life of the their countries of origin while carving out a space for livelihoods and cultural activity beyond the borders of any one nation.

Castles and Miller claim that:

> It is important to realize that all (these) movements have common roots, and that they are closely interrelated. Western penetration triggered off profound changes in other societies, first through colonization, then through military involvement, political links, the Cold War, trade and investment. The upsurge in migration is due to rapid processes of economic, demographic, social, political, cultural and environmental change, which arise from decolonization, modernization and uneven development. These processes seem set to accelerate in the future, leading to even greater dislocations and changes in societies and hence to even larger migrations.
>
> (Castles and Miller, 1993, p.165)

International migrations, while often closely related to political circumstances, and while they have historically been frequently forced or involuntary, are also crucially linked to processes of immanent and intentional development.

As Castles and Miller suggest, many of the causes of international migration are related to social and economic development. Development also causes migrations within countries, including urbanization (which we will discuss at greater length in Section 4 below). Migration in turn contributes to the potential for development in the country of destination – and labour remittances from migrants have become a crucial part of some countries' foreign exchange earnings.

These are very general observations, which attempt to cover a huge and diverse range of human movements. Each migration flow we have discussed has a complex history, with significant and different consequences for the countries of origin and destination, not to mention for the individuals concerned, and the local areas they have travelled from and to. We have noted how national immigration policies have partly responded to changing economic conditions, but they have also been deeply influenced by racist and xenophobic sentiments in receiving populations. Defensive immigration policies are one of the crucial ways in which contemporary states continue to be significant international actors, and to reinforce the borders which define their territories. Global human migration flows might be one of the defining features of contemporary globalization, but they also exemplify the complicated implications of these flows for patterns of territorialization, especially at the scale of the nation-state.

The following section continues to explore this theme, of the relationship between human displacement and territorial entities, especially nation-states and localities, by looking in detail at one specific collective migration, from Bangladesh to the United Kingdom.

3.2 Journeying: from Sylhet to London

<u>Activity 8</u>

Read the case study of migration from Sylhet to London below. As you do so,

(a) think about the different forces which have shaped this particular migration across the globe; and

(b) note any mention of the different 'territorializations' or scales discussed in Section 2 above: local, national and global.

(c) What role does each of these scales play in shaping the migration patterns?

Case study: from Sylhet to London

In the East End of London, a local urban development initiative has taken the name, 'Banglatown'. Around 40 000 Bangladeshi people live in the London borough of Tower Hamlets, one of the poorest in the country. While most of the Bangladeshi families in the neighbourhood are relatively poor, there are a number of successful business enterprises along a well-known street, Brick Lane, which has become famous across the city for its restaurants and shops trading in South Asian goods, serving the local population and communities across the city (Figure 3.3). The neighbourhood is also closely juxtaposed with the City of London, one of the wealthiest areas in the entire country, home to the major finance houses and the Bank of England (Figure 3.4). City workers form a ready market for the local restaurants, and in the context of a relatively multicultural political climate, the marketing of the area around Brick Lane as Banglatown is designed to extend its attraction to city workers, Londoners and tourists alike.

Alongside the globally connected financial houses in the City of London, a substantial community of Bangladeshi people has been established in a neighbourhood which has long been home to immigrant communities, such as the French Huguenots and later Jewish settlers. The links and connections from Tower Hamlets once again span the globe, this time linked to one of the poorest countries in the world, Bangladesh, and even more surprisingly, to a relatively small region within that country.

Of the Bangladeshi people now living in Britain, 95% have their origins in one area in Bangladesh – Sylhet.[*] Although people from Bengal have been involved in trade and overseas travel for hundreds of years, this particular group of villages came to have an extraordinarily strong link with the United Kingdom – such that villages in the region with many migrants in the UK are called *londoni* (Figure 3.5).

[*]This narrative has been drawn substantially from Katy Gardner's (1995) study, *Global Migrants, Local Lives*.

Figure 3.3 Restaurants and street markets in Brick Lane, 'Banglatown', London.

Figure 3.4 View of the City of London from Tower Hamlets.

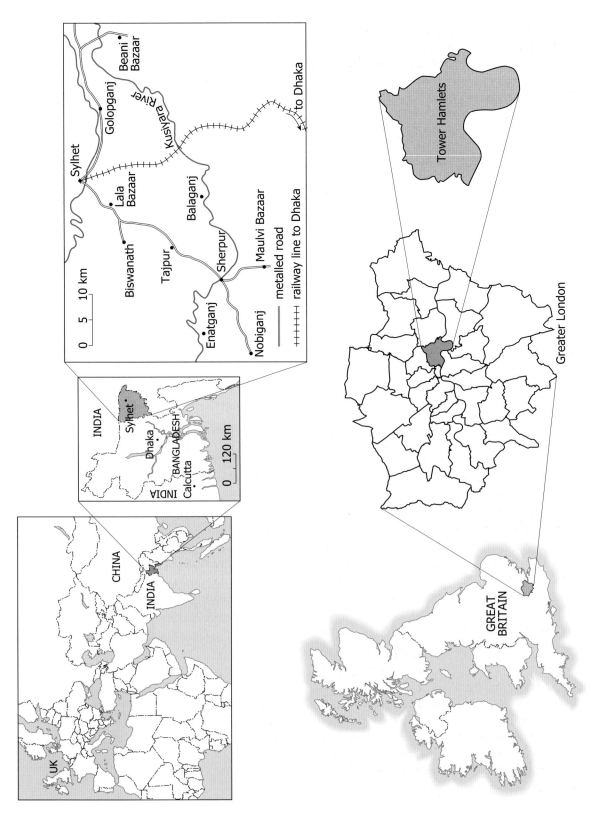

Figure 3.5 Links between London and Tower Hamlets to/from 'londoni' villages in Sylhet and Bangladesh.

Sylhet is several hundred miles from the Bay of Bengal, with no particularly easy access to the sea port of Calcutta, although in the wet season cargo ships are able to access the region. Yet it became a major source area for men to find work on British ships as *lascars* or sailors; these subsequently formed the nucleus of migrants to the UK. How did this come about?

One of the pre-conditions is the long-standing foreign trading links from the region. In this case, these were primarily with the British, who had been trading in the region through the East India Company since the mid-eighteenth century. There had also been substantial in-migration to the area as a result of the developing tea industry. The resources and cash crops of the region had been valued for trading purposes for centuries, but with the emerging colonial economy by the twentieth century, there was increasing value placed on the cheap labour also available in the region. In Sylhet, a large proportion of the farmers were independent land-owners, and in her study of migration from the region Katy Gardner suggests that migration might have been stimulated by increasing competition over land in the region, in a context of a predominance of relatively independent-minded farmers, seeking to maintain their autonomy.

With sufficient surplus wealth to pay for the papers and fares required to work on the British ships, and the flexibility to lose the labour of one or more family members, circumstances were more favourable for migration out of this region than in other neighbouring areas, and migrants usually came from richer or middle-income rural families. As members of the Commonwealth, potential migrants at that time could stay and work in the UK for as long as they wished. Numbers were relatively small, encouraged by the first successful sailors, and only increased in the early 1960s as factory work and formal systems of recruitment for industrial jobs became more common. Once again, though, it was links to existing migrants, usually family members, which both encouraged and facilitated people's movement. As Gardner notes, 'social networks and people's relative access to them has been vital in determining who does and does not migrate. ... Once a few men had taken the plunge, geographically specific networks developed and a pattern of movement towards Britain began to emerge' (pp. 45–46).

However, although these networks enabled access to British-based brokers, employees and accommodation, changes in the immigration legislation relating to the Commonwealth in 1971 made entrance to the United Kingdom more difficult. Limited increasingly to family reunion and skilled employment, migration has now tended to cause substantial differentiation in the local economy in Sylhet between migrant and non-migrant communities. While initially there was the opportunity for some poorer, even landless, households to better their position through access to employment in the UK, social differentiation in villages in Sylhet is increasingly occurring along lines shaped by differential access to foreign employment, in addition to long-standing divisions based on land-holdings. With this closing down of access to the UK, increasing numbers of families are investing in sending migrants to the Middle East, often relying on expensive intermediaries and brokers, and frequently without the protection of legal documentation. Despite the substantial costs and risks involved, Gardner suggests that the 'communal fantasy' of plenty in these foreign lands is so powerful that 'many households are prepared to risk their land in the hope of gaining access to it' (p.63).

The significance of migration in Sylhet has meant that a valuing of local land and social networks (*desh*) has been extended and changed by the valuing of foreign connections (*bidesh*) and the resources which these have introduced into local life in Bangladesh. But Gardner draws some important conclusions about how *desh* and *bidesh* – or local places and migrant flows – are related. Firstly, she indicates that it is local context, together with local social ties and networks, which have shaped the possibility of migration for different families. Family members already in the UK draw in relatives to opportunities that they have access to, or in earlier times, ensured access to rare jobs on passing ships. *Desh* has shaped the engagement with *bidesh*. Secondly, *bidesh* has introduced many changes in *desh*, but this is not a one-way street. Resources, commodities and the potential of *bidesh* may be valued, but flows are the other way too. Migrants often take with them products from home, valued because local food and land are seen as particularly powerful and enriching. *Bidesh*, though, has become a powerful source of mystical fantasy and wealth, in contrast to the poverty of *desh*. Home and abroad are closely intertwined, through constant flows of family and goods, through imaginative relations, and because each continues to shape the other. Remittances, for example, are usually used to buy land, enhancing the local standing of migrant households. Increasingly, 'the village population can be classified not in terms of access to land, but instead in terms of access to foreign countries' (p. 81).

Things change, of course, and Gardner suggests that while links between British members of Sylhet households and family members still in Bangladesh may continue to be strong today, over time this is likely to diminish. And while migration for wealthier households to the UK, and more recently to the Middle East, often helped strengthen the family's position, for poorer, landless households, accessing foreign employment often leaves people in debt, and sometimes even worse off than before. The meaning of migration, as well as that of home, is not static, and neither is their relationship. But most importantly, home and abroad are not separate from each other, but as Gardner notes, 'migrants are part of two worlds which are dynamically intertwined' (p. 6).

Comment

Very briefly touched on in the case study is the variety of earlier globalizations and global links which laid the basis for the twentieth century labour migrations which form the focus of the study. However, while the broader set of processes of trade and colonization set in train certain opportunities for employment and movement, there were quite specific circumstances which enabled the migrations from Sylhet to London. And as Katy Gardner mentions, 'the transformations ... [described] here are the result of local dynamism and self-reliance' (p. 20). Individual men, successfully gaining access to work as sailors, taking the initiative to explore employment in London, and passing on information and contacts to relatives and friends, played a major role in establishing the global links between *londoni* and London. Moreover, the local social relations of property and family in the region made migration a feasible option.

The case study, then, while tracing one of many migration links between places around the world, reminds us of the very specific social and historical circumstances which made that particular trajectory possible. Although the myriad movements of people around the world might add up to a 'global' phenomenon, it is important to bear in mind the contingent and contextual basis of each choice to move, and different routes of migration. 'Flows' happen in and through particular parts of the world, trace specific and often hard-won channels across the globe, and influence and shape distinctive places in the process. It is also important to realize that local dynamics are not simply overrun by the impacts of globalization. Experiences in Sylhet villages shaped the engagements and meanings of migration, just as much as the villages were transformed by their strong connections with other places.

Furthermore, it was *national immigration policies* which at first enabled and then stopped the movement of people to London, and it was the specific *local conditions* of the Sylhet villages which made the move to London possible and determined what particular form it would take. And of course these movements are deeply personal, bound up not only with individuals willing to take risks or follow friends and relatives, but also bound up with dreams, hopes and fantasies about distant places and possible futures.

Visually, it is striking to think of the trajectory of movement from Sylhet to London as cutting across the territorializations or scales which we noted have shaped development (look again at Figure 3.5). Cutting across national boundaries and tying the world of Bangladeshi villages to neighbourhoods of East London, *migration trajectories carve a specific route across the globe – and each specific link is deeply implicated in both nation and locality.*

The migration experience ties two localities together in the experiences and imaginations of the migrants. As Gardner notes, London and Sylhet became 'different locations of the same society' (p.8), and migrants 'part of two worlds which are dynamically intertwined' (p.6). The social context of the migrants becomes stretched across the distance of the migration trajectory; the 'local' is recreated in the imagination and in voyages back and forth, constructed as a composite of personal and household experiences out of physically distant places.

3.3 Migration and development: development out of place?

If aspects of development thinking and practice have been closely tied to territorializations like local areas and nation-states, phenomena like international migration pose some important practical and intellectual challenges. Cutting across scales which seem to matter in relation to many other aspects of development, and yet clearly shaped by these same entities (the local, the nation-state), *experiences of 'displacement' like migration call into question the close association between bounded territories and development.* Changes in Bangladeshi villages were effected through employment and social life in places like London and Saudi Arabia, and Bangladesh as a country has actively encouraged migrant labour as a way of covering foreign exchange requirements crucial to development programmes. *The flows of migration have come to be as crucial for development as the nationally based plans and projects of the national state.* There are clearly important questions to be asked about 'where' development interventions can best be made in the context of transnational networks.

The case study poses further problems for the territorializations or scales we outlined in Section 2. We might ask 'where' is *the local*, for example, and suggest that as in the migrants' experience, the local was much wider in scope than the physical limits of the village in Bangladesh or the neighbourhood in East London. And while the migration could be thought of as part of *'globalization'*, it also involved specific links and trajectories: it was not something 'out there' existing at some planetary scale, but something produced and shaped by particular social relations in particular places or along certain routes. Finally, *the state*, while important in shaping migration, was itself also influenced by these flows, including, for example, the colonial links which encouraged the immigration of labourers with consequences for long-term questions of national identity and economic potential in Britain and Bangladesh. However, more recently the British state has also been determined to defend its boundaries against continuing migration, confounding the idea that globalization has undermined state powers and influence and instead suggesting that it has contributed to the reconstruction (sometimes through force) of the boundaries of states. In the example above it was apparent that *places and the mobile trajectories or flows of migrants are closely bound up with each other.* Flows don't necessarily undermine the distinctiveness of places, and it is often the unique history of a place, like Sylhet, which is responsible for encouraging human movements.

In this section we have been focusing on one form of transnational flow, that of human migration. In the first section of this Introduction, though, we identified 'displacements' more broadly as being as much to do with the flows of resources, things or ideas as they are to do with human movements. Part 2 of this Theme will explore some of these other kinds of displacements in more detail (the conclusion to this Introduction outlines what will be covered in Part 2). However, it is worth recalling, as noted in Section 1, that even if people don't move anywhere, their experiences of a range of flows and links affecting that place can be dislocating. In Section 2 we noted that 'places' are produced by a range of social and economic processes, flows and networks, some of which stretch across the globe. We referred briefly to the example of white British people, who might feel displaced by a range of political and cultural changes, such as the post-Second World War labour migrations. A recent UK-based commission on multiculturalism, for example, noted a range of such changes, including devolution, globalization, Britain's standing in the world, changes in gender relations, and 'the principal subject matter of the report – the recognition that England, Scotland and Wales are multi-ethnic, multi-faith, multicultural, multi-community societies. Each of these changes involves dislocations in the way people see themselves, and in how they see the territorial, political and cultural space – Britain – where they meet, and where they seek to build a common life' (Commission on the Future of Multi-Ethnic Britain, 2000, p.2).

Places, then, the people and communities in them and their well-being and future development are at least partly shaped and changed as a consequence of their links to wider flows and networks. We could say that *'places' are created and transformed through all kinds of 'displacements', flows of people, ideas and resources.* However, sometimes places are so thoroughly changed that their previous social meaning is completely erased – when whole villages become submerged in new dams, for example, or absorbed into high-rise urban developments. While migrants from Sylhet found new ways of making a living in the United Kingdom, they maintained links with their families and some people chose to move back and forth from one place to the other. Sylhet was certainly transformed by this movement – but it remained recognizable as a place with reciprocal relations between villages in Bangladesh and households in England. In other situations, especially in circumstances of forced removal, the consequences of displacement can be more severe: forced to leave their homes, individuals, families and communities may have to completely re-establish themselves in another place, with none of the links and support back to their place of origin.

Many forms of *forcible displacement* are a result of conflict or political repression but, as we noted in Section 1, development itself has also posed a great threat to many settled communities. Attempts to address the social and economic consequences of forcible removals highlight how in particular places, households and communities build livelihoods as well as social and kinship networks which can facilitate exchanges of all kinds. Relocated, often with severe disruptions to livelihoods and social networks, many such communities experience great difficulties. If the costs of development are not to be unjustly imposed on locally affected communities, appropriate policies need to be adopted, and these need to appreciate the many different ways in which being located in a particular place can be crucial to livelihoods and to social life.

In this light, the plight of forcibly displaced people, forced to abandon their homes and the places where local networks enabled access to social and political rights and membership of communities and household networks, poses a serious challenge to humanitarian assistance and intentional development ambitions (Kibreab, 1999).

In an era when mobility and displacement are often celebrated as sources of opportunity, the experience of forced displacement reminds us of the value and significance of place and locality.

The challenges to development thinking and practice posed by the significance of flows, networks and displacements ironically bring us back in this final section to reflect on how it is that *being in place still matters*. As we noted in Section 1, flows of all kinds, including human movements, may have both positive and negative outcomes. A large-scale urban development in Bombay (Mumbai) – itself a response to increasing flows of people and economic activity into the city – caused many local inhabitants of the area to lose access to their livelihoods and to the social networks and ties on which they had depended. Unlike the migrants from Sylhet, the villagers on the outskirts of Mumbai, described in the case study below, found their displacement to make way for urban expansion a devastating experience.

The following section explores the experience of *development-induced displacement*. It looks more closely at the idea of the 'local' and why places are important in *livelihoods and development opportunities*. It also considers how the severely dislocating effects of development displacements can be ameliorated. It does this through an account of development-induced displacement in Mumbai and considers:

- why the displacement was seen as necessary;
- what steps were taken by the authorities to ameliorate the consequences of removal;
- what other agents played a role in shaping the outcomes;
- how future development-induced displacements might benefit from a stronger appreciation of how places and livelihoods are entwined.

Summary of Section 3

1 International migration flows have changed over time, at least partly in relation to processes of immanent development

2 Territorializations like states and local communities are important in shaping the direction and nature of human migration, both forced and voluntary

3 Flows like international migration cut across local and national scales, potentially undermining them, but also playing an important role in re-shaping both states and local communities

4 Just as places, or territorializations, have been the basis for much development practice and thinking, 'displacements' like human migration have important consequences for development.

4 Development-induced displacement: the case of urban development in Mumbai/Bombay*

*The city has been renamed Mumbai, as it was originally called after the goddess Mumba Devi (the patron goddess of the original inhabitants), which was corrupted to the Portuguese 'Bombaim' and English 'Bombay'. We will refer to the city wherever possible as Mumbai, except in relation to some historical events which took place while the city was called Bombay, or where official documents or names at the time refer to Bombay.

Nowhere are the dilemmas of intentional development more apparent than in cases of development-induced displacement. In order to advance plans for the economic growth, or well-being, of a region or a country, a smaller group of people may have to be uprooted. The challenge is to ensure that they do not suffer the risk of impoverishment due to their resettlement. If the consequences of such forms of displacement are to be ameliorated (see Chapter 2 of the Course Book, on development as ameliorating the consequences of economic growth), the dynamic relationship between people's livelihoods and the places in which they live needs to be understood more clearly. This may not remove the need for hard choices, but it might help ensure that some people don't suffer unnecessarily in order for others to advance.

These choices about development and displacement are posed very starkly in large, rapidly growing cities. With more and more people living in large cities, the need to provide services and housing can mean that those living on the periphery of rapidly expanding cities, for example, are in danger of being displaced. Add to this the restless process of profit-driven property development and the threats to settled, poor communities, especially those occupying land illegally, are severe. The following section looks at one example of this in Mumbai, where villagers were expected to make way for the rapidly expanding city. First, we briefly survey the urbanization process in India which made the displacement of local villagers seem necessary for development of the city.

4.1 Urbanization in India: managing human displacement

Although India's urban population of 217.61 million in 1991 is greater than the total population of many countries as a whole, it has only about 26% of the country's population living in urban areas, and is one of the least urbanized countries in the world. In fact, in 1991 India ranked 58th in terms of percentage of urban to total population out of 83 low income and lower-middle income countries (World Bank, 1993). Nonetheless, most observers agree that the urban population is growing rapidly. The fastest recorded urban population growth rate of 46.14% was attained in the decade 1971–81, when the average annual *natural* rate of increase of the urban population (i.e. births minus deaths) was only 19.3% (Table 4.1). *Most of the growth in India's cities in these decades was due to in-migration, rather than natural growth of the existing population.*

Table 4.1 Average annual birth rate, death rate and rate of natural increase per 1000 persons in India 1971–80 and 1981–90

Period	Rate	Urban	Rural
1971–80	Birth rate	28.5	35.8
	Death rate	9.2	15.8
	Rate of natural increase	19.3	20.0
1981–90	Birth rate	27.1	34.1
	Death rate	7.6	12.5
	Rate of natural increase	19.5	21.6

Source: For 1971–80, *Census of India, 1991*, Paper 2 of 1991, Provisional Population Totals: Rural–urban Distribution. For 1981–90, *Sample Registration Bulletin*, January, 1995, vol. 29, no 1, Registrar General of India, New Delhi.

Activity 10

Look at Table 4.2 below. Take particular note of the last two columns and assess the changes over time in the extent and rate of growth of urbanization. Is urbanization accelerating or slowing down?

Table 4.2 Urbanization trends in India

Census years	Total population	Urban population	Number of towns	Percentage of urban population to total population	Urban growth rate over the decade (%)
1901	238 396 327	25 851 873	1827	10.84	0.09
1911	252 093 390	25 941 633	1815	10.29	0.35
1921	251 321 213	28 086 167	1949	11.18	8.27
1931	278 977 238	33 455 989	2072	11.99	19.12
1941	318 660 580	44 153 297	2250	13.86	31.97
1951	361 088 090	62 443 709	2843	17.29	41.42
1961	439 234 771	78 936 603	2365	17.97	26.41
1971	548 159 652	109 113 977	2590	19.91	38.23
1981	683 329 097	159 462 547	3378	23.34	46.14
1991	846 302 688	217 611 012	3768	25.71	36.47

Note: Population numbers include projected populations of Assam in 1981 and Jammu and Kashmir in 1991.

Source: *Census of India 1991*, Paper 1 of 1992, Vol II, Final Population Totals.

Comment

The proportion of urban to total population increased in every decade during the century, as did the rate of growth of the total urban population until the last decade recorded, 1981–91 (apart from 1951–61). Compared with the previous decade (1971–81), urban population growth declined sharply by 10% to 36.47% in 1981–91. So until this decade, the pace of urbanization had generally been increasing. Why has it apparently slowed down?

Most observers agree that the rate of urbanization has in fact not slowed down, and they have suggested a number of explanations for the observed trends in the data in Table 4.2, which suggest otherwise. These all have to do with the expansion of most cities beyond their defined borders – so the problem is that *places are still being considered rural when in fact they have already been urbanized.* Fewer new towns have been created in recent years, leading to an increasing concentration of population in rural areas adjacent to large urban centres. Also, large numbers of people, particularly new in-migrants, are in fact choosing to reside in peripheral rural areas and commute to the nearby large cities owing to the high cost of living and high levels of congestion and pollution prevailing in the cities. Hyderabad, Pune (originally known as Poona), Bhopal, Jaipur and Chandigarh are cities whose peripheral countryside has experienced sizeable in-migration. It takes some time for the statistical definition of a city's borders to catch up with this kind of urban sprawl, so the effect of excluding these peripheral areas from the definition of a city, or what is termed in India an 'urban agglomeration' is an *underestimation of rural–urban migration.* This is compounded by a probable under-enumeration of the urban population.

In fact, India's cities have been expanding so rapidly that they have attracted a range of policy interventions to try to limit this growth. Government and urban planners had been hoping that the growth in large cities would slow down after they had adopted specific policies to achieve this – but most commentators agree that this has been to no avail. India's industrial policy prohibited further concentration of industries within urban areas and new industrial firms in the private sector were not allowed to locate within 25 km of a major urban centre. The aim was to encourage industrial development to deconcentrate to smaller towns and reduce the growth of large cities. *This policy did not lead to a reduction in the growth of large cities, but it did accentuate the process of sub-urbanization, or urban sprawl* (which caused the under-count of the urban population), by inducing non-agricultural activities in the adjacent rural hinterland of cities. The pressure on cities to expand, and especially to encourage development on the outskirts or in nearby rural hinterlands, provides the context for the case study of development-induced displacement in Mumbai which follows. *Rural people in these areas are under great pressure to give up their land and their livelihoods to urban growth.*

Political leaders also considered that improved living conditions in rural areas would reduce rural–urban migration. A series of policies and programmes were introduced to promote the agricultural sector and to address rural poverty. The official statistics indicate a dramatic decline in rural poverty incidence from 54% in 1972–73 to 40% in 1983–84 and 33% in 1987–88 (Planning Commission, 1993). It is thus quite plausible that various agricultural and rural development programmes have had some impact in reducing rural poverty and may have led to a decline in the 'push' factors associated with rural–urban migration. On the whole, though, it is generally agreed that the apparent slow-down of rural–urban migration in India is not directly attributable to governmental efforts of agricultural rural development, or its policies of industrial dispersal. Rather, much of it is because urban sprawl in the past two decades has not been captured adequately in the demarcation and enumeration of urban agglomerations.

Of greater concern to most policy-makers is assessing *future trends in urbanization*. Although there have been attempts to slow urban growth in the past (with little effect), *new industrial and trade liberalization policies*, which are opening India to the global economy, *are now expected to accelerate the pace of industrial and economic growth*. These policies are likely to influence the spatial pattern of urban growth. Larger cities with better infrastructure will attract most of the inward investments, causing even greater concentration of economic activities and urban population. The likely urban pattern as a result of the economic liberalization will be increasing concentration of activities in and around the 23 metropolitan cities of India. Rapid growth of urban population could also lead to much higher national levels of urbanization – about 36% in 2001 and about 46% in 2011 (Statistical Outline of India, 1994–95). India's total urban population is projected to be 365 million in 2001 and 530 million in 2011. Cities are perceived as gateways to the globalization of India's economy and the growth in the formal tertiary or services sector in metropolitan economies is expected to be most rapid.

In all, and despite the trends in Table 4.2, the magnitude of rural–urban migration in India is set to increase between 1991 and 2011. As India's premier commercial centre, Mumbai is likely to experience these pressures of globalization and urbanization most intensely.

4.2 The challenges of urbanization: issues and problems facing Mumbai

Mumbai is the richest city in India, accounting for over a third of the country's tax revenue (for a short profile of the city of Mumbai see Box 20.4 on p.440 in the Course Book). This makes it an attractive destination for the landless and dispossessed, not only from the state of Maharashtra (India's most industrialized state of which Mumbai is the capital) but also from all over the country. It is the centre of India's industry, and the centre of its financial life. With a population of 12.6 million in 1991 and estimated to be 15–16 million in 2001, Mumbai ranks first in the nation and sixth among the world's largest metropolises in terms of population.

A fishing village in the sixteenth century, Mumbai was ceded by the Moguls to the Portuguese in the 1630s. It became part of the dowry of Catherine of Braganza on her marriage to King Charles II, and was leased by him to the East India Company in 1688 for ten pounds a year. With Calcutta, it became one of the principal trading port cities for the British as it has a superb natural harbour. Its true rise to prominence awaited the building of the railways and the expansion of cotton growing in the hinterland from the 1860s. It was proudly hailed as the primary city in India, and the second largest city in the British Empire after London. In less than three centuries of British patronage, Mumbai grew phenomenally from an insignificant group of villages to the largest city in western India, and a metropolis of national and international importance (Figure 4.1).

(a)

(b)

Figure 4.1 Mumbai (Bombay): colonial past, international future. (a) High-rise buildings at the gateway to India. (b) Victoria Terminus: a relic of Bombay's colonial history.

Figure 4.2 Location of Mumbai and New Mumbai. (a) The surrounding rail links. (b) The urban-industrial corridor stretches from Mumbai to Pune.

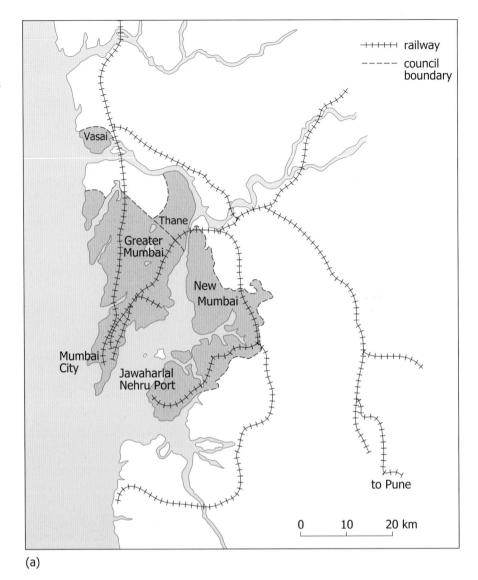

(a)

The city's growth has been marked by the outward dispersion of people and activities, particularly along two transport axes (and around the stations along the railway line) to the north to Vasai and to the north-east to Thane (Figure 4.2a). Industrial expansion has given rise to an urban-industrial corridor stretching 64 miles between Mumbai and Pune (Figure 4.2b). With the industrial saturation of Mumbai City, the spillover of economic activity has been directed northward, through the Greater Mumbai area.

Mumbai, the state of Maharashtra, and in fact the entire country have benefited tremendously from the city's economic progress and wealth. Mumbai's story, however has not only been one of progress and prosperity, but increasingly includes serious urban deficiencies and congestion. Some of the most visible features are problems of shelter

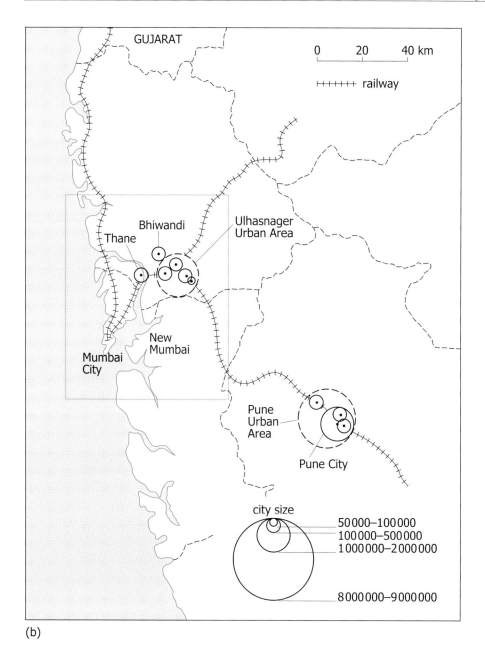

(b)

(housing), transportation and insufficient basic services and infrastructure for the growing population. Mumbai's poorest inhabitants have arguably suffered most from the negligible amount of public housing, from the highly insufficient supply of potable water, from the absence of a properly working sewerage and sanitation system, from poor education and health facilities, and from an absurdly overcrowded commuter transportation system. But the economic progress of the city as a whole has been hampered, and middle classes have also faced severe problems in obtaining adequate housing and services (see Box 4.1).

Box 4.1 Some challenges of urbanization in Mumbai

Formal housing

Associated with the shortage of adequate housing and rapid urban growth are rising land prices. Mumbai is currently one of the most expensive cities in the world in terms of land value. Scarcity of land led to a low supply of additional new housing (Figure 4.3a) and new formal housing is mainly constructed in the extended suburbs and satellite towns, far from places of work. This has resulted in a shift of population northwards and created long daily commutes on extremely overcrowded suburban trains.

Chawls

Four out of five low-income households were accommodated in *chawls*, mostly dilapidated one-room dwellings of a size not larger than 15 m², with shared facilities such as toilets, staircases and access corridors, and only partially provided with potable water or functioning public latrines. In 1989, such *chawls* made up nearly 75% of total formal housing stock in Greater Mumbai, whereas the all-India average of one-room tenements amounted to 50% (Sundaram, 1989, pp.59–63). The average number of persons per household living in such *chawls* was found to be 6.3, but could go up to as much as 20 to 40 people in one unit. One toilet had, on average, to be shared by six dwellings (ibid, pp.61–63). Nearly four out of five households are living in slums (Figure 4.3b). Between 1961 and 1981 the number of people living in slums increased nearly six times, from around 700 000 to over 4 million (National Commission on Urbanization, 1987).

Pavement dwellers

Those who do not even have the resources to live in a slum are living on the pavement. About 97% of households living on the pavement include earners, who sustain the city economy in several ways and who contribute to the municipal revenues (Sundaram, 1989, pp.65–66).

Water

By 1986, 72% of all households living in formal housing were supplied with water for only 5 to 6 hours per day, and the remaining 28% for only 3 to 5 hours per day. By the late 1980s at least 4 million people were getting their water from standpipes, with an average of 270 persons per pipe (Sundaram, 1989, p.59) (Figure 4.3c). In general, the extended suburbs and low-income settlements are worst in terms of services. Squatters that are not officially recognized (as is mostly the case) may have illegal connections to water pipes or to the electricity network. According to the Mumbai Municipal Corporation figures, the number of deaths due to infections and parasitic diseases was during the 1980s an astonishing 40% of total deaths, many of them related to unclean water or bad sanitary conditions (Sundaram, 1989, p.60).

Figure 4.3 Living in Mumbai: (a) formal housing; (b) tenements; (c) standpipes; (d) suburban railway line.

Transport

Besides housing and the provision of basic urban services, transportation has increasingly become a major problem. The pressure on the road and railway system has become so high that it has become one of the main bottlenecks for the city economy and a heavy burden on Mumbai's millions of daily commuters. One of the major factors contributing to the transportation problem is Mumbai's peculiar geographical shape as a narrow peninsular running north to south, with two of the three main centres of work being located in the southern part of the city. At present, the two suburban railway lines (Figure 4.3d) and public buses together carry about 5 million passengers every day (Pasricha, 1994). In 1995, 250 000 private cars and 34 000 taxis were also competing for space on Mumbai's clogged roads (Statistical Outline of India, 1994–95, p.209).

These severe problems, already evident in the 1960s, demanded a clear policy response. The city authorities turned to policies popular with cities and planners all over the world – decentralization and dispersal of economic activity and the population from the overcrowded city were adopted as the central themes for future urban development. A new metropolitan centre was proposed, involving the development of a twin metropolis on the mainland. This new urban centre, adjacent to the existing city, would provide the advanced infrastructure necessary to attract employment-intensive tertiary activities and also provide social, cultural and other amenities for the surrounding area. But the area designated for development was not empty. The authorities responded to one sort of crisis of 'displacement' – rapid urbanization consequent upon global and national flows of people and goods – by initiating development which was to require further 'displacement' of villages, livelihoods and social networks in surrounding areas. This was to create serious problems for some residents, even as it hoped to solve the problems of millions of others.

4.3 Urban development and displacement – implementing the Twin City Plan

In 1964, the first Development Plan for Greater Bombay for the period 1964–81 presented by the Municipal Corporation of Greater Bombay argued that future urban growth should be carefully directed, to stop the flow of migrants to Bombay from occupying land badly needed for industrial or commercial purposes. The idea of developing a twin city called 'New Bombay' (Jacquemin, 1999) to decongest Greater Bombay was born. Located opposite the Bombay peninsular on the mainland, partly reclaimed from the low-lying marshy land and linked by a newly constructed bridge, New Bombay has, since the early 1970s, been planned to become an independent twin city of comparable size to the initial metropolis (see Figure 4.2a).

The Development Plan envisaged the creation of a new technologically advanced Jawaharlal Nehru Port. The project also aimed at shifting the wholesale market sector (e.g. iron and steel, onion and potatoes, grains, pulses, sugar, spices) from the old city to the twin city. The aim was to reduce the urban and economic pressure on Mumbai, divert new incoming migrants towards the edges of the city and relieve some of the existing urban problems in the centre such as housing shortages and the lack of infrastructure for the development of industries and business. Land on the mainland, to be acquired from peasants and fisherman, was conceived as a crucial primary resource for the development of New Bombay.

The government of Maharashtra designated an area of 343.7 square kilometres for the new city. It was estimated that it would affect 156 000 people (24 878 households) (Jacquemin, 1999) living in the area, including some 95 villages. Of these villages, 33 were to be completely displaced, that is, they would lose all land and houses, and 62 villages were to lose all agricultural and common lands. The fully displaced villagers were to be given alternative sites to build new houses (Parasuraman, 1999, p.121).

The government founded the City and Industrial Development Corporation (CIDCO) to administer the development of New Bombay. CIDCO was responsible for acquiring, developing and disposing of land throughout the project area in order to achieve the goals and priorities of the twin city development project.

Activity 11

On the basis of what you have read so far, make a note to yourself as to who you think was likely to benefit from the development project and who was likely to lose out? Keep this in mind as you read on.

(Comments on this activity will be found after Activity 12)

Implementing this large urban development scheme inflicted substantial social costs upon the villagers. Over time these have become more visible and have generated conflicts and tensions. To develop this new town and its infrastructure, it was decided that more than 12 000 of the households living in the 95 villages in the area (who were mainly engaged in agriculture, fishing and saltpan labour) were to be displaced. Over half of the land was privately owned by a large number of families and about a third was publicly owned, so the development entailed large-scale land acquisition from local land-owners and various compensation agreements. People engaged in saltpan work on government land, those engaged in fishing, landless people and self-employed people were not awarded any compensation for the loss of their livelihoods as they did not own any land. Those who lost less than one acre (a large number of households) were also not eligible for compensatory employment with the New Bombay project.

The Jawaharlal Nehru Port was originally obliged to provide employment for every displaced household that had land, but less than 33% of those households ultimately obtained employment. Employment in the port was available only to educated or technically skilled people. The port's obligation to provide employment for all displaced households was found to be not legally binding. People who could not obtain employment with the port or other industries in the area took recourse to various non-agricultural wage labour activities (loading, unloading and other contractor-related activities in port and port-related establishments, sand extraction or related casual wage labour). The difficulties in replacing lost economic opportunities were compounded by the influx of migrant labourers working for contractors. Contractors preferred migrant labourers because they were subservient, were willing to live in camps and worked for less than the minimum wage. Some local people prevented contractors from hiring migrant labourers by attacking the labour camps.

As the plans have progressed over the years more and more land has been acquired for development, and in retrospect the compensation has been very poor. Those who can afford it have taken the government to court while others, who cannot, reluctantly accept the money, or mobilize protest movements. Some received compensation immediately while others had to wait for several years. Those who had owned no land, but depended on local resources and networks for their livelihoods, especially those engaged in fishing activities, village artisans, tribal and landless agricultural labourers or saltpan workers, have officially never been considered as affected people by the project.

Compensation of a sort – in monetary form and agreed employment – had therefore been offered to affected people in this example of displacement. But, inadequate as these might have been, many villagers were not eligible for them. It is exactly these people who had most to lose from the removals.

In the project-affected area, caste groups such as *Agris* (salt-makers), *Kolis* (traditionally, communities of fishermen and sailors) and *Karadis* (cultivators of rice) accounted for 98% of the population. All these are 'backward communities' in the government of India classification of caste groups. Thus it was the most poor and vulnerable people who were displaced from these villages and communities. Very few households owned saltpans as most saltpan land belonged to the government. All saltpan lands were lost to the development. *In the post-displacement period all these communities lost access to the source of their livelihood and, in being displaced, also lost access to their community networks.*

In assessing the consequences of development-induced displacement, though, there are wider ramifications and a longer time horizon to consider. *Kolis* were landless people in the area dependent on access to the sea to earn their livelihood. Women handled the sale of fish. Due to a sharp increase in chemical pollution in the coastal area as a result of the developments, the fish population has disappeared. To enter deeper waters, more advanced equipment is needed and special permits are required, both of which are too expensive for most traditional fishermen. Consequently over time fishing as a profession has almost been wiped out. Moreover, the consequences of intense industrial development have increased environmental pollution, leading to illnesses such as malaria, bronchitis, pneumonia, burning of eyes, etc. Although villagers' livelihoods were tied to the affected localities in many different ways, compensation and employment schemes were directed at the loss of formally owned property only and failed to address the loss of access to common property resources, such as the saltpans, or the consequences of longer term damage to the environment.

Very little compensation has been offered to the former villagers in terms of social or cultural facilities to replace what they have lost, and their place-dependent livelihoods affected both directly and indirectly by economic changes have suffered irreparable damage. Few of the promises regarding alternative employment and assistance with rehabilitation in new locations have actually been implemented. Rehabilitation schemes initially introduced to assist people with re-establishing livelihoods were soon abandoned and the poorest villagers have had to leave the area. Those who stayed face grave problems with basic utilities such as water and sewerage, causing many sanitary and health problems.

The Development Plan for this project very positively stated that the villages were to be kept intact, encouraging the process of absorption of the rural population into the new urban setting, enabling full and active participation as a community in the new forms of economic and social life. But the costs of living in an urban area (food, education, transportation, medical expenses, and all kinds of taxes and services) have increased many times, and most people have spent their compensation on meeting these routine expenses. More than that, low-income housing project areas, where villagers were resettled, have seen about three-quarters of the original households replaced by higher income groups as the costs of housing and living in the area have risen.

Involuntary displacement involves unravelling established human collectivities and existing patterns of social organization, including production systems and networks of social support. The removal of the fishing community disrupted social and economic networks. New urban development resulted not only in the community being physically deprived of living space but also, through pollution and development, it destroyed long-standing ways of making a living. Loss of livelihood involved separation from occupations with which families might have been associated for generations. In doing so, it also challenged the sense of identity which people in the community had developed over a long period of time. At times of vulnerability, like resettlement, social networks can acquire a heightened importance, and the disruption to those networks entailed by physical displacement and loss of livelihood and associated identities can create a damaging sense of social displacement. As Cernea and McDowell (2000, p.7) note, 'home rebuilding … is only a first step in culturally identifying with the new location and in reconstructing the social fabric of the new communities.'

Activity 12

Compare your thoughts from Activity 11 with the above discussion of the villagers' experiences of removal. What else do you think could have been done to ease the transition for displaced communities?

Comment

Displacement in India and elsewhere has often been handled in a contentious way, and has often generated resistance from displaced communities, as in the international campaign against removals needed to build the Narmada dam. Similarly, in Mumbai protests at forced removals have been common, suggesting that the affected communities feel their treatment has been inappropriate. The account so far might suggest that the developers and the government should have paid greater attention to the loss of livelihoods associated with the local environment, especially to the loss of more informal livelihood strategies which wouldn't automatically qualify for monetary compensation. Lack of attention to the longer-term consequences of the development project, for example environmental degradation, suggests that the scope of concern with development-induced displacement also needs to stretch across time. But the opportunity to engage local communities in generating alternative development paths might also be considered. Although the development of the twin city project in Mumbai was a top-down initiative, the local community did not simply acquiesce. Protests over compensation have emerged over the years, demanding greater consideration of people's losses. They have also had an impact on the legal requirements for compensation and rehabilitation of livelihoods associated with future developments.

Urban planners, NGOs and academics in Greater Mumbai joined villagers to oppose the proposed displacements. They assisted community protestors with financial support, petitioned government ministries and political leaders, organized public lectures and campaigned against the applications of Mumbai residents for housing in New Bombay. This campaign reduced the demand for housing in New Bombay on the part of Mumbai residents, resulting in shortage of funds for investment in the housing development (Parasuraman, 1999, p.122).

The Peasants and Workers Party (PWP) also strongly opposed the New Bombay project from the point of view of those expecting compensation for loss of their land. This led to delays in land acquisition for the project. After prolonged contestation, CIDCO reached a settlement with the leaders of PWP in 1979, fixing the price of land at Rs.15 000 per acre (Verma, 1985). But continued resentment of the proposed level of compensation led to the founding of the *Jamin Bachao Samiti* (Save the Land Committee), to unite the project-affected people in their struggle for better compensation. In 1984 as the land acquisition process intensified, the opposition movement had become quite strong, and people demanded a compensation of Rs.40 000 per acre. Many meetings were held with the CIDCO officials and the government of Maharashtra, but no settlement could be reached. The police force was deployed to restrain people at protest rallies, and police action killed five people. In February 1984, the government, *Jamin Bachao Samiti* and CIDCO officials reached a compromise and agreed a basic compensation of Rs.27 000 per acre plus a grant of Rs.3000 per acre, although the amount paid per acre varied according to the quality of the land and trees on the land (Parasuraman, 1999, p.123).

There were many active groups and organizations at the community level trying to 'empower' marginalized sections of the community in relation to displacement. They lobbied government and agencies through political channels in order to influence upcoming decisions that affected the communities, such as decisions about compensation and provision of alternative land for rebuilding houses. These confrontational approaches challenged the government, through campaigning against a policy or by direct action in the form of street protest.

While displacement can seriously deplete social capital, especially in the form of dense local networks and associations, these campaigns and protests were one way in which citizens drew on these networks as well as wider associations across the city to organize themselves and represent their interests. Powerful governments and private sector developers can be brought to task, then, and communities facing displacement can refuse to bear the social costs of development projects which benefit the wider community or a few entrepreneurs. Further afield, governments and developers are under increasing international pressure to abide by clear guidelines for ensuring that development projects do not contribute to impoverishment.

Activity 13

In the light of the Mumbai twin city project experience, can you suggest how an understanding of the significance of place in development could inform future compensation or rehabilitation plans in cases of development-induced displacement?

Comment

'Displacement' is not easily compensated by a straightforward economic transaction, a simple substitution of property with money. It also involves 'resettlement', i.e. the process of physical relocation of those displaced and their socio-economic re-establishment as family/household micro-units and as larger communities. It requires 'rehabilitation', i.e. the restoration of lost economic and social capabilities. Formal procedures of compensation and rehousing need to be accompanied by careful consideration of the kinds of livelihood strategies and community networks which sustained households, especially the poorest. Michael Cernea expresses some of the dislocating effects of displacement on social and economic networks which communities establish in particular places:

> Forced displacement tears apart the existing social fabric. It disperses and fragments communities, dismantles patterns of social organization and interpersonal ties; kinship groups become scattered as well. Life-sustaining informal networks of reciprocal help, local voluntary associations, and self-organized mutual service are disrupted. This is a net loss of valuable 'social capital' that compounds the loss of natural, physical and human capital. The social capital lost through social disarticulation is typically unperceived and uncompensated by the programs causing it, and this real loss has long-term consequences.

(Cernea, 2000, p.30)

The rehabilitation and resettlement policy in Mumbai failed to compensate for the loss of common resources – saltpans and fishery – which had previously been a source of livelihood. People lost access to both these resources after the establishment of the port, without compensation. All *Kolis*, and the majority of *Karadis* and *Agris*, were thus devastated economically. Development projects neither recognized the rights of people to the common resources nor helped people to switch to other income-generating activities compatible with their skills and expertise. The region is the most rapidly industrializing area in the country. However, the project-affected people, being fishing communities and saltpan workers, were ill equipped to take advantage of the growing industrial employment opportunities.

This case study highlights how urban development agencies in India (and elsewhere) have obtained substantial powers to direct land use in cities. In this case, the land acquired was far in excess of the amount required for the present and future needs of the port (Verma, 1985). The unused land is now being handed over to private sector builders for large-scale housing projects catering to the needs of workers in the area. This has led to massive speculation by private developers, pushing up the cost of land by 240% and cost of houses by 350% within one decade, especially since liberalization in 1991. The intervention by the Government of India and the state government in redefining land-use patterns has been to the detriment of the traditional communities such as the fishermen and peasant cultivators of the area. The real beneficiaries were the speculators, developers, builders, bureaucrats and the planning and executing bodies. Alternatives might have been sought which paid attention to the diversity of development needs in the newly urbanizing area, and which might have sought more environmentally sustainable forms of development, thus preserving existing livelihood possibilities, like fishing, for future generations.

While most countries have elaborate policies and programmes to promote economic growth, often little attention is given to the problems of displacement attendant upon that growth. As Cernea (2000, p.12) notes, 'Development will continue to require changes in land use and water use and this make various degrees of population relocation at times unavoidable. Yet, this does not mean that the inequitable distribution of development's gains and pains is itself inevitable, or ethically justified'.

Summary of Section 4
1 Rapid rates of rural–urban migration and increasing globalization of economic activity place substantial development pressures on large cities.
2 Displacement frequently accompanies urban development projects.
3 Plans to ameliorate the effects of development-induced displacement need to go beyond monetary compensation.
4 Common property resources and informal livelihoods need to be considered.
5 Place-based economic and social networks making up 'social capital' need to be protected, or replaced.

5 Conclusions

5.1 Development and displacement

This Introduction has presented you with ways of thinking about a set of processes involving movements and flows which we have argued have increasingly come to be part of the concerns of development agencies, and which have accompanied processes of both intended and immanent development. Human movements (both voluntary and forced) have formed the focus of the case studies which we have explored – international migration from Sylhet to London, and development-induced displacements in the Greater Mumbai area. But we have also used the term 'displacements' in a wider sense to refer to the mobility of ideas and resources as well as people. As we noted, feelings of dislocation and displacement can occur in place, as much as they can emerge as a result of actual movements. And places in general are shaped by wider external forces, composed of all sorts of flows, of goods, money, cultural practices and laws.

The broadest conclusion which we have reached in this text, then, is that *if we are to study displacement, we need to have a good understanding of place too.* For, as we discovered, places and displacements, or territories and flows, are intricately bound up with one another. A flow is not simply movement. In the case of humans especially, it involves travel, a particular route, a mode of transport, a set of cultural practices of return and maintaining contacts. And territories, like villages and states, are very much a part of the flows, shaping their direction, frequency and impacts and in turn being transformed by these movements.

The three territories we have been discussing – the local, national and the global – are all socially produced, and therefore change over time. The image of flows cutting across these territories encourages us to embrace the many different translocal and transnational phenomena which feature in the contemporary world, as we reframe development to meet current challenges. But it also encourages us to look at the mutual interactions of flows of all kinds and the institutions and identities associated with territories. Institutions like the state are changing – deterritorialization of states may be part of the experience of globalization, but re-territorialization, the refounding of states on new premises and through new activities, is also provoked. Re-constituting territories and re-establishing forms of located identity, such as local governments or ethnic belonging, can be an important way of trying to regain some collective control over the various flows and networks which can have such disruptive, as well as potentially positive, impacts on places and social groups.

In this Introduction we have begun the task of establishing a framework and developing a vocabulary with which to make sense of the range of phenomena associated with displacement which are of concern to international development thought and practice. Part 2 of this Theme will take these further. (At that time you will have a choice between studying *Displacement* or *Sustainability*). Building on the analytical approach developed in this Introduction, the Theme book *Development and Displacement,* and the associated study guide will explore examples of displacement which are currently challenging and transforming approaches to development. There we will consider in some detail how development is changing in the face of displacements, with new agendas and new agents of development increasingly evident.

The book will consider four examples of displacement and their implications for development, and the introduction and conclusion to the book will support and reinforce the analysis and concepts which we have covered in this Introduction. The four examples to be studied are:

1   *Forced displacement and the nation-state.* The central theme of the chapter will be the way in which forced international migration and development-induced displacements are crucially shaped by the nation-state. Without taking for granted the distinction between 'forced' and voluntary' forms of migration, it will focus on the challenge which forced migrations present to the nation state both conceptually and empirically. A key issue will therefore be the relationship between the figure of the refugee, falling outside the nation-state system, and the continuing importance of the nation-state in framing international responses to the 'problem' of refugees. The way in which the figure of the refugee came into being within the field of an international system of states will be explored. 'Resettlers', forcibly displaced by state-led development initiatives, similarly pose a threat to the nation-state, highlighting its often fraudulent claims to represent all citizens equally. International efforts to intervene in situations causing both refugees and resettlers point to the limitations of defining human rights on the basis of the nation-state and raise much wider issues concerning the ethics of global citizenship.

2   *Diaspora and development.* As the movement of people, either forced or voluntary, is breaking down our traditional, territorially based understandings of 'nation', 'community' and 'citizenship', communities are becoming increasingly transnational. The chapter will investigate the ways in which development happens through the creation of diasporic relations, and also how the existence of diasporic and transnational communities might change development practices. The chapter will consider:

(a)   *Development in the diaspora*: how people within diasporic communities use their localized diasporic connections to secure economic and social well-being and, as a by-product, contribute to the development of their locality. This is diasporic development in place.

(b) *Development through the diaspora*: how diasporic communities utilize their diffuse global connections beyond the locality to facilitate economic and social well-being. This is diasporic development through space.

(c) *Development by the diaspora*: how diasporic flows and connections back 'home' facilitate the development – and, sometimes, creation – of these 'homelands'. This is diasporic development across space.

The chapter will focus on the example of the African diaspora, in addition to better known case studies from other parts of the world.

3 *City futures: new territories for development studies?* Urbanization has crept to the top of the agendas of many international development agencies. With about half the world's populations now living in cities, and most of the world's largest mega cities in the poorest countries, their future development poses many challenges. The chapter will explore the consequences for urban development of an approach to cities which sees them as distinct places, yet constituted out of many different flows and networks of people and resources. In the contemporary period of globalization, when links across and between cities are arguably becoming more crucial to development, the need to build up city identities as the foundation for future growth, and to negotiate across diverse interests, individuals and communities in the process, suggests that it is important to keep in mind that cities are both distinctive (political and economic) territories, and sites of connections elsewhere (displacements). Within the context of globalization, structural adjustment and decentralization, the focus of urban development in many poorer countries has shifted from infrastructural developments and service delivery within the city, to a concern with the *development of the urban economy within the context of global links and flows*. This chapter will provide a framework for the potential economic futures of cities in line with recent changes in the policy environment and wider economic and political trends.

4 *'Think local, act global': transnational networks and development.* The increasing number and scope of social movements and NGOs represents a shifting of loyalties that can no longer be contained (however much they ever were) within national boundaries or confined to localities. One such example is Amnesty International. There are over one million Amnesty International members, committed to human rights issues, in 160 countries. This 'shrinking political distance' has resulted in domestic issues increasingly appearing on international agendas. Awareness of the injustices and

needs of 'distant strangers' has been an impetus for establishing connections and allegiances beyond the state. In this sense, experiences of displacement (or in this context, often referred to as 'scaling up') can have positive meanings for development in that groups may now have opportunities to effect change concerning their lives in different ways and at different scales than they did before. Thus, opportunities due to changing technologies are emerging for groups that want to influence the process of change at a global scale. These groups could act as potential vehicles for transporting alternative visions of development from the local to the global level through transnational NGO coalitions. The chapter explores the rise of global networking within and amongst transnational NGOs and social movements.

We hope you will find this interesting, and wish you good luck as you make your choice of which Themes to study in Part 2.

References

African Development Report 2000 (2000) Oxford University Press, Oxford, for the African Development Bank.

Allen, T. (ed.) (1996) *In Search of Cool Ground: War, Flight and Homecoming in North-East Africa*, UNRISD, Geneva.

Allen, T. and Thomas, A. (eds) (2000) *Poverty and Development into the 21st Century*, Oxford University Press, Oxford in association with the Open University, Milton Keynes. (Course Book)

Castles, S. and Miller, M. J. (1993) *The Age of Migration: International Population Movements in the Modern World*, Macmillan, London.

Census of India (1991), Paper I, Vol. I & Vol. II, Final Population Totals.

Cernea, M. (2000) 'Risks, safeguards and reconstruction: a model for poulation displacement and resettlement', in Cernea, M. and McDowell, C. (eds) (2000) *Risks and Reconstruction: Experiences of Resettlers and Refugees*, The World Bank, Washington DC.

Cernea, M. and McDowell, C. (eds) (2000) *Risks and Reconstruction: Experiences of Resettlers and Refugees*, The World Bank, Washington DC.

Chambers, R. (1998) 'Paradigm shifts and the practice of participatory research and development', in Nelson, N. and Wright, S. (eds) *Power and Participatory Development*, Intermediate Technology Publications, London, pp.30–42.

Commission on the Future of Multi-Ethnic Britain (2000) *The Future of Multi-Ethnic Britain*, The Runnymede Trust, London.

Crehan, K. (1997) *Fractured Community: Landscapes of Power and Gender in Rural Zambia*, University of California Press, Berkeley.

Crush, J. and Veriava, F. (1998) *Transforming South African Migration and Immigration Policy*, Southern African Migration Project, Cape Town.

Curtin, P. (1997) 'Africa and global patterns of migration', in Wang Gungwu (ed.) *Global History and Migrations*, Westview Press, Boulder, pp.63–94.

Fox, J. (1996) 'How does civil society thicken? The political construction of social capital in rural Mexico', *World Development*, vol.24, no.6, pp.1089–1103.

Friedmann, J. (1992) *Empowerment: The Politics of Alternative Development*, Blackwell, Oxford.

Gardner, K. & Lewis, D. (1996) *Anthropology, Development and the Post-modern Challenge*, Pluto Press, London.

Gardner, K. (1995) *Global Migrants, Local Lives: Travel and Transformation in Rural Bangladesh*, Clarendon Press, Oxford.

Gupta, A. (1998) *Postcolonial Developments: Agriculture in the Making of Modern India*, Duke University Press, London.

Gupta, A. and Ferguson, J. (1999) *Culture, Power, Place: Explorations in Cultural Anthropology*, Duke University Press, London.

Hannerz, U. (1996) *Transnational Connections: culture, people, places*, Routledge, New York.

Hassner, P. (1998) 'Refugees: a special case for cosmopolitan citizenship?' in Archibugi, D., Held, D. and Kohler, M. (eds) *Re-imagining Political Community: Studies in Cosmopolitan Democracy*, Polity Press, Cambridge, pp.273–286.

Hirst, P. and Thompson, G. (1996) *Globalization in Question*, Polity, Cambridge.

Holland, J. and Blackburn, J. (1998) *Whose Voice? Participatory Research and Policy Change*, Intermediate Technology Publications, London.

Jacquemin, A. R. A. (1999) *Urban Development and New Towns in the Third World: Lessons from the New Bombay Experience*, Ashgate, Aldershot.

Kibreab, G. (1999) 'Revisiting the debate on people, place, identity and displacement', *Journal of Refugee Studies*, vol.12, no.4, pp.384–410.

Leftwich, A. (2000). *States of Development*, Polity, Cambridge.

Massey, D, (1995) 'The conceptualization of place', in Massey, D. and Jess, P. (eds) *A Place in the World?*, Oxford University Press, Oxford, pp.45–86.

Mohan, G. and Stokke, K. (2000) 'Participatory development and empowerment: the dangers of localism', *Third World Quarterly*, vol.21, no.2, pp.247–268.

Morawska, E. and Spohn, W. (1997) 'Moving Europeans in the globalizing world: contemporary migrations in historical perspective (1955–1995 vs 1870–1914)', in Wang Gungwu (ed.) *Global History and Migration*, Westview Press, Boulder, pp.23–62.

Parasuraman, S. (1999) *The Development Dilemma: Displacement in India*, Macmillan, Basingstoke, in association with Institute of Social Studies, The Hague.

Pasricha, P. S. (1994) 'Pathway to privatization', *The Sunday Free Press*, 13 November 1994.

Planning Commission (1993) *Report of the Expert Group on Estimation of Proportion and Number of Poor*, Government of India, New Delhi.

Roy, A. (1997) *The God of Small Things*, Flamingo, London.

Sack, R. (1985) *Human Territoriality*, Cambridge University Press, Cambridge.

Statistical Outline of India (1994–95) Tata Services Limited, Department of Economics and Statistics, Bombay.

Sundaram, P. S. A. (1989) *Bombay, Can It House its Millions?* Clarion Books, New Delhi.

Verma, H. S. (1985) *Bombay, New Bombay and Metropolitan Region: Growth Process and Planning Lessons*, Concept, New Delhi.

World Bank (1993) *World Development Report 1993*, Oxford University Press, New York.

Acknowledgements

Grateful acknowledgement is made to the following sources for permission to reproduce material within this book:

Text

Pages 29–32: Crehan, K. (1993), *The Fractured Community: Landscapes of Power and Gender in Rural Zambia,* University of California Press. Copyright © 1997 The Regents of the University of California; *pages 43–44:* Hadland, A., 'Reviled street traders declared good for the economy', *Sunday Independent,* South Africa; *pages 50, 53–54:* © Katy Gardner 1995. Reprinted from *Global Migrants, Local Lives: Travel and Transformation in Rural Bangladesh* by Katy Gardner (1995) by permission of Oxford University Press.

Figures

Figures 1.1, 1.2, 1.3, 2.2, 2.3 and 3.1: Howard Davies/Exile Images; *Figure 2.1:* Adapted from Taylor, P. J. (1993), *Political Geography,* Longman Group, UK Limited. Reprinted by permission of Pearson Educational Limited; *Figure 2.4:* Adapted from Crehan, K. (1993), *The Fractured Community: Landscapes of Power and Gender in Rural Zambia,* University of California Press. Copyright © 1997 The Regents of the University of California; *Figure 3.2:* Castles, S. and Miller, M. J., *The Age of Migration International Population Movements in the Modern World,* 1993, The Macmillan Press Limited, reproduced with permission of Palgrave. The Guildford Publications, Inc.; *Figure 3.3 (a):* www.britainonview.com, *Figure 3.3 (b) and 3.4:* courtesy of Jenny Robinson; *Figure 3.5:* based on map 1.3, *Global Migrants, Local Lives: Travel and Transformation in Rural Bangladesh* by Katy Gardner (1995) by permission of Oxford University Press; *Figures 4.1 and 4.3:* © Vandana Desai; *Figure 4.2 (a):* Thorner, A. and Patel, S., (1995), *Bombay: A Metaphor for Modern India,* reproduced by permission of Oxford University Press, New Delhi, India; *(b):* Kosambi, M. (1986), *Bombay in Transition,* Almqvist & Wiksell International. © 1986 Meera Kosambi.

Tables

Tables 4.1 and 4.2: Census of India, 1991, Office of the Registrar General of India, New Delhi.

Every effort has been made to contact copyright owners. If any have been inadvertently overlooked, the publishers will be pleased to make the necessary arrangements at the first opportunity.

The Course Team

ACADEMIC STAFF

Joanna Chataway, *Co-Chair and author, Technology and Knowledge*

Jenny Robinson, *Co-Chair, co-ordinator and author, Displacement*

Gordon Wilson, *Co-Chair, co-ordinator and author, Sustainability*

Simon Bromley, *co-ordinator and author, Transitions*

Will Brown, *co-ordinator and author, Transitions*

Pam Furniss, *author, Sustainability*

Tom Hewitt, *co-ordinator and author, Technology and Knowledge*

Hazel Johnson, *co-ordinator and author, Poverty and Inequality*

Bob Kelly, *assessment strategy and author, Study Guide to the Course Book*

Maureen Mackintosh, *author, Transitions*

Judith Mehta, *author, Transitions*

Stephen Peake, *author, Sustainability*

Sandrine Simon, *author, Sustainability*

Alan Thomas, *author and co-editor of the Course Book*

Richard Treves, *author, Sustainability*

David Wield, *critical reader*

Helen Yanacopulos, *co-ordinator and author, Technology and Knowledge*

BBC STAFF

Jenny Bardwell, *Series Producer July 2000–May 2001*

Gail Block, *Audio Producer*

Giselle Corbett, *Production Manager*

Phil Gauron, *Series Producer*

Julie Laing, *Series Personal Assistant*

Andrew Law, *Executive*

Jenny Morgan, *Freelance Director*

Claire Sandry, *Audio Producer*

Mercia Seminara, *Audio Producer*

SUPPORT STAFF

Carolyn Baxter, *Course Manager*

Sylvan Bentley, *Picture Researcher*

Philippa Broadbent, *Print Buying Controller*

Penny Brown, *QA Software Testing Assistant*

Daphne Cross, *Print Buying Co-ordinator*

Sue Dobson, *Web Designer*

Tony Duggan, *Learning Projects Manager*

Peta Jellis, *Course Manager July–November 2000*

Alison George, *Web Designer*

Richard Hoyle, *Graphic Designer*

Lori Johnston, *Editor*

Roy Lawrance, *Graphic Artist*

Cathy McNulty, *Course Secretary*

Katie Meade, *Rights Editor*

Lynda Oddy, *QA Software Testing Manager*

Pauline O'Dwyer, *Course Secretary*

Katharine Reedy, *Library Online Adviser*

Janice Robertson, *Editor*

John Taylor, *Copublishing Manager*

Mark Thomas, *Team Leader, Online Applications Web Team*

Pamela Wardell, *Editor*

EXTERNAL ASSESSOR

Dr K. Bezanson, *Institute of Development Studies, University of Sussex*

CONSULTANTS

Tim Allen, *author and co-editor of the Course Book*

Seife Ayele, *Poverty and Inequality*

Jo Beall, *Sustainability*

Flemming Christiaansen, *Transitions*

Ben Crow, *Sustainability*

Vandana Desai, *Displacement, and Study Guide to the Course Book*

Wendy Fisher, *Technology and Knowledge*

Leroi Henry, *Study Guide to the Course Book*

Ann Le Mare, *Preparing for Development*

Giles Mohan, *Displacement*

Paul Mosley, *Poverty and Inequality*

Njuguna N'gethe, *Study Guide to the Course Book*

Wendy Olsen, *Poverty and Inequality*

Ruth Pearson, *Poverty and Inequality*

Judith Scott, *Poverty and Inequality*

Laixiang Sun, *Transitions*

John Taylor, *Transitions*

David Turton, *Displacement*

Marc Wuyts, *Transitions*

CRITICAL READERS

Henry Bernstein, *Transitions*

Tenkai Bonger, *Sustainability*

Jessimen Chipika, *Poverty and Inequality*

Rachel Marcus, *Poverty and Inequality*

Martin Reynolds, *Sustainability*

Rafal Rohozinski, *Technology and Knowledge*

AbdouMaliq Simone, *Displacement*

WEB TESTERS

Alan Brown, Jackie Bush, Christine Cubbitt, Andrew Dakers, Sarah Downham, Alan Foster, Anna Mattarollo, Fahmida Muhit, Eric Needs, Wendy Shaffer, Nigel Shakespear, Phil Talman

U213
International Development: Challenges for a World in Transition

Course texts

Introduction to Transitions

Introduction to Poverty and Inequality

Introduction to Technology and Knowledge

Introduction to Displacement

Introduction to Sustainability

Transitions

Poverty and Inequality

Technology and Knowledge (web-based)

Displacement

Sustainability